Straight talk about small business

Other Books by the Author

How to Pick the Right Small Business Opportunity
How to Be Your Own Management Consultant
The Handbook of Business Problem Solving (Editor-in-Chief)

Straight talk about small business: What other books don't tell you about the pitfalls and profits of starting and managing your own business

Kenneth J. Albert

McGraw-Hill Book Company

New York   St. Louis   San Francisco   Auckland
Bogotá   Hamburg   Johannesburg   London   Madrid
Mexico   Montreal   New Delhi   Panama   Paris
São Paulo   Singapore   Sydney   Tokyo   Toronto

Library of Congress Cataloging in Publication Data

Albert, Kenneth J, date.
Straight talk about small business.

Includes index.
1. Small business—Management. 2. New business
enterprises—Management. I. Title.
HD69.S6A37   658'.022   80-17656
ISBN 0-07-000949-X

34567890   MUMU   8987654321

The editors for this book were Robert A. Rosenbaum and Tobia L.
Worth, the designer was Mark E. Safran, and the production
supervisor was Sally Fliess. It was set in Souvenir by David E.
Seham, Inc.

Printed and bound by The Murray Printing Company.

To my sons, Bruce Albert and Ken Albert

Contents.

Preface.

I believe that most of us want "straight talk." We respect a boss who levels with us. We appreciate friends who speak up when honest differences develop. We long for politicians who say what they think, rather than say what they think we want to hear.

I believe that people interested in becoming business owners also want "straight talk." They want to know about the risks as well as the rewards. They want to understand the disadvantages as well as the advantages. They want to know about the pitfalls as well as the opportunities. They want a straightforward, unbiased presentation of the facts so that they can make intelligent choices and sound decisions. That's what this book is all about.

Straight Talk Provides Answers

One of my primary goals in writing this book was to produce a balanced and thorough perspective. This allows the reader to answer critical questions:

- Should I, in fact, become a small business owner?
- What is the operating reality and outlook for the most popular small business types (e.g., mail order, retailing, restaurants, manufacturing, that great idea, and service businesses).

- Why is starting a business from scratch not always the best choice?
- What are the ins-and-outs of buying a franchise or an ongoing business?
- What do I need to know about financing?
- How do I optimize the use of lawyers, accountants, insurance agents, and other advisers?
- What are the best ways to cope with recordkeeping, government regulations, and taxes?

Straight Talk Increases the Probability of Success

If you do decide to enter the world of the self-employed, material in this book (that has never appeared in any other small business book) will imporve your chances of success:

- Clearly spelled out are the reasons why many new businesses succeed (and why others don't).
- Entry strategy alternatives that minimize risk are described and detailed.
- A whole chapter is devoted to techniques needed to overcome common hazzards and pitfalls.
- The last chapter explains how selling leads directly to success.

I Believe in Small Business

In our unsettled and less and less predictable economic climate, there are three truths that speak strongly for the small business option:

1.   Small business in an essential and large segment of our economy and of our way of life. There are over 3.5 million successful small businesses in the United States.

2.   The best investment one can make in life is to invest in oneself. Ben Franklin put it this way: "If a man empties his purse into his head, no one can take it away from him."

3.   The best job security is not to have a job at all, but rather to be self-employed.

I'm emphasizing these points here because I don't want talk of "risk" and "disadvantages" and "pitfalls" to scare anyone away from a possible career in small business. I'm not a crapehanger. And this is not a gloom and doom book. What I'm saying is that there are hurdles and detours. And that knowledge is the best weapon in overcoming them. Sure, there are problems. Nothing worthwhile comes easy. But operating a small business can be one of the most fulfilling and financially rewarding experiences in life.

Thanks again to Carol and Mrs. V. for their typing. And thanks to McGraw-Hill for believing that there is a need and a market for *"straight talk about small business."*

Ken Albert

Aptos, California

ONE

Straight talk: an introduction.

You've seen them. Books with titles like *1001 Surefire Businesses You Can Start with Loose Change—and Make $1 Million in Your Spare Time.* They're the "promise them anything" books about small business. They are filled with happy talk and fantastic success stories. And they are success stories in themselves—often smashing best sellers.

On the other hand, some books about small business almost defy you to read them. These come in two formats: 600-page "tomes" that read like economics textbooks and the "entrepreneur" books that use complex words to expound on everything from private placement venture capital to optimizing your corporate structure. Although both tomes and entrepreneur books have some value, it's almost impossible for the typical new businessperson to benefit from them.

It's very tempting for an author to write a book about small business that is overly optimistic—to promise abundant success. After all, would a diet book that doesn't assure quick, easy weight loss succeed in bookstores? And it's just as tempting for an author to allow his or her expertise (be it finance, new ventures, or whatever) to dominate the content of a book.

My aim in writing this book has been to avoid these shortcomings.

1

I have strived to be realistic, honest, and straightforward. And I have done my best to concentrate on information that is useful to the largest number of readers, especially information that has been intentionally deleted from "happy talk" small business books. I'm going "to tell it like it is," as Howard Cosell says.

80 PERCENT FAILURE—YET MILLIONS OF SUCCESS STORIES.

Probably the most widely publicized statistic about small businesses relates to the failure rate of new small businesses. According to the Small Business Administration (SBA) statistic, 80 percent of new businesses (4 out of 5) fail within 5 years. Not very encouraging, is it? Some experts claim that the figure is too high, that it's actually closer to 60 percent. But even 60 percent isn't good: it says that over half of all startups fail. Not very good odds.

But there is another, much more hopeful, set of statistics. Take a look at these U.S. Department of Commerce numbers for ongoing small businesses:

- 2.4 million established retailers with sales of less than $1 million a year
- 420,000 small wholesalers
- 450,000 franchised small businesses
- 400,000 manufacturers with annual sales of less than $1 million

These numbers represent an awful lot of success stories—over 3.5 million success stories. And the data are even more impressive when we consider that most of these businesses were started and are being successfully run by ordinary people with ordinary talents.

It's undeniably true that most people who start businesses fail. But it's also undeniably true that there are literally millions who have succeeded. And the men and women who will succeed in the future are the ones who say to themselves "If they did it, damn it, I can do it too. I'm just as good as anybody else." It's the corny old positive mental attitude (PMA) philosophy that's been preached for years by the self-made insurance tycoon, W. Clement Stone. It's corny, but it works. Determination and self-confidence contribute to success.

Many book publishers and booksellers are convinced that most people who buy books about small business are dreamers—dreamers who will never even attempt to start a small business. I don't agree. I think that most buyers of small business books have serious intentions. They are considering their career options and looking for answers. Some look and decide not to leap. That's fine. Not everyone is cut out to be self-employed. Others look and do leap. Of these, some fail. But a failure in a small business venture is not the end of the world, especially if little capital is risked and job security is not threatened. Recently, I read about a Chicago purchasing agent who started a used-car appraisal business with just that attitude. He and a partner pooled $1,500 from their savings accounts and started the venture without quitting their jobs. In a recent newspaper interview the purchasing agent said, "If it fails, I've lost some time and $750. Big deal. But if it flies, I'm on my way!"

Failure can also prepare one for success at a later date. Many successful people have failed on their first try. Also, failure, if nothing else, shows that one at least had the gumption to try.

Getting back to statistics. There is one encouraging failure statistic. Less than 20 percent of new franchises fail. Chapter 3 has much more on the reasons for small business successes and failures. Down-to-earth methods of minimizing risks are emphasized.

WHAT IS THE FUTURE OF SMALL BUSINESS?

Quite simply, the future of small business in the United States is good. My reasoning for this outlook goes like this. The SBA classifies over 90 percent of all businesses in this country as small. This says that our economy depends on small business. That's impressive to begin with. But the giant multinational companies are growing and eating up smaller, weaker competitors all the time. So just because 9 out of 10 businesses now are small doesn't, in itself, foretell a prosperous future for small business.

What does suggest a healthy outlook for small business is the irreplaceable nature of the products and services they provide, and the inability of large companies to compete.

First, let's look at the nature of the output of small business. Small businesses are the *exclusive* providers of a list of products and services that is almost never ending. Here's just a sampling I developed by browsing through the yellow pages:

- Florists
- Home remodeling
- Furnace/AC repair
- Ambulance services
- Answering services
- Antique shops
- Auto body repair
- Automobile dealers
- Barber shops
- Travel agencies
- Carpet cleaning
- Pet shops
- Cleaners
- Contractors
- Delivery services
- Radiator repair
- Equipment rental
- Kennels
- Firewood
- Charter fishing

- Formal wear rental
- Gift shops
- Hobby shops
- Instant printing
- Janitorial services
- Chinese restaurants
- Landscaping
- Lawn mower repair
- Tuck-pointing
- Nursery products
- Sandblasting
- Pest control
- Photography
- Plumbing
- Real estate sales

Just think what it would be like to live in a community without small businesses. Literally hundreds of products and services would be unavailable. No haircuts. No emergency plumbing repairs. No kennels. Imagine your community's main business district. Take away the small businesses, and not much would be left.

This is why I'm bullish on small businesses. They are essential to our way of life. And in most cases, you don't have to worry about big business pushing out small businesses. Their very bigness makes them incapable of competing effectively in many segments of our economy. And their new venture expansion policies almost always excludes their getting involved in *small* businesses. I know of one Fortune 500 company, for example, that won't look at a new venture unless it promises to generate $100 million in revenue each year!

It's also interesting that the growth and expansion of big business often creates business opportunities for small business. That's called the umbrella effect. Many small businesses prosper by supplying products or services to the big companies—products and services that the big guys don't have the time or efficiency to provide for themselves.

It almost goes without saying (but I'm going to say it anyway) that the outlook for small businesses varies greatly by business type. Independent fast-food operations (that are competing with major national chains like McDonald's) and full-service gasoline stations (that compete with the likes of Aamco, Midas, Sears, K-Mart) are just two types of businesses that have poor outlooks. What this says is that a small business opportunity must be selected carefully and methodically. Chapters 5 to 7 explain how to do this. My appraisal, based on extensive research, of the outlook for the most commonly started businesses is presented in detail in Chapter 4.

THE SMALL BUSINESS KNOWLEDGE GAP.

Did you have a course in high school (or even in college) that dealt with starting a small business? Did one of your high school or college counselors, or one of your parents, suggest that maybe you should prepare yourself to run your own business some day? Have you learned very much in your years of employment that would prepare you to run a small business successfully?

Most likely, your answer to all these questions is no. And that's the reason there is a gap in our knowledge about small business. Most schools don't offer courses related to running a small business, and they don't train people to be self-employed. The only obvious exceptions are the professions—accounting, law, and medicine. Even in these, I know that *more* lawyers and accountants work for large firms or large corporations than are self-employed. And most business schools are geared to training students to be specialized employees of big business. I have an M.B.A. degree from a prestigious business school, for example, but what I learned there that helps me as a self-employed person you could put in a thimble. So, I've had to educate myself.

Society—including parents, teachers, friends, and counselors (mostly, by the way, *employees*) always seem to put emphasis on "getting a good job." Then, when you do get a good job, or embark on a career of two or three jobs in succession, you discover that in most cases the experience you're gaining doesn't apply to running your own business. Big business is a world of specialists—food chemists, repair technicians, internal auditors, market planners, plant managers, and credit and collection staffers. It rarely provides the experience useful in small business. Many people work in big business for decades and never write a business letter or talk to a customer!

What I'm leading up to is that you shouldn't feel inadequate if you don't know a lot about starting and running a business. Not many people do. Our educational institutions, society, and big business have seen to that. But if you have any hopes of succeeding in your own business, you've got to work hard to fill your education gap. The very fact that you're reading these words is encouraging. Read anything and everything you can. Get acquainted with persons who own small businesses. And seek out the few opportunities for formal education that do exist in small business. Some business schools are now offering a course on the topic, as are some junior colleges. Throughout this book I'll be pointing out other options that are available for increasing your knowledge and expertise.

CAPITAL REQUIREMENTS.

Chapter 9 is devoted exclusively to the realities of financing a small business. But I do want to say a little in this first chapter about capital requirements. The amount of capital required to start a business can vary anywhere from less than $500 to more than $500,000.

I've frequently heard people explain that they can't start a business because they don't have the money to invest. And what's more, they say, they have tried to borrow money and were turned down. People who talk like that are just making excuses. Many businesses can be started with very little capital. Why not start one, make some money, and then invest this profit in a larger, more desirable business? Then you will have established a track record of business success, a track record that will qualify you for a business loan.

A major cause of failure in small business is insufficient working capital. Never start a business unless you have sufficient capital. But don't use insufficient capital as an excuse for not starting some type of business.

ASSESSING YOUR PROSPECTS.

Many studies have been done to define the characteristics that it takes to succeed in a small business. Results suggest that successful businesspersons:

- Are determined to succeed
- Are willing to take moderate risks
- Recognize and take advantage of opportunities
- Exhibit objectivity when making tough decisions
- Consider money as a measure of accomplishment, not as an end in itself
- Are good at planning ahead
- Want to know how they are doing (feedback)

Fortunately, these characteristics are similar to what it takes to succeed in *any* career. Job success takes determination, moderate risk taking, exploiting of opportunities, objective decision making and on and on. So if you've had a successful career record as an employee, it bodes well for you.

IT'S NOT EASY.

"Working for someone else. That's the easy way." So speaks a self-made man who has run a successful independent clothing store for over 20 years.

"Could you explain what you mean?" I asked.

"I work long hours. I have a hell of a time finding and keeping good people. My tailor just quit because I wouldn't pay him in cash. I get hit on all the time by local organizations to contribute time or money, or to buy an ad in this program or that booklet. It's not easy."

"Well then, why do you do it?"

"For a lot of reasons. The money is good. I know I'm accomplishing something. I control what I do. And it makes me feel good to be my own man. But it's not easy, and don't believe anyone who tells you it is."

Our clothing store owner's message is simple. It's hard work, but to the owner it's worth the effort. You'll have to decide if it's worth it to you.

DECIDE FOR YOURSELF.

This book will help you find out if a small business is for you. You'll read about the good—the money you can make, the self-satisfaction, the freedom to set your own work schedule, the tax advantages, business opportunities with proven success records, attractive startup strategies, proven marketing approaches, etc. But you'll also discover the negatives. I'm not going to pull punches.

Then you can ponder it yourself. Examine the good. Examine the bad. You'll have the material necessary to make a wise choice. And you'll know a lot about the ins and outs of of running a successful business.

TWO

Risks and rewards.

This is the kind of chapter that some might say will kill the sale of a book about small business. "People don't want to read about the negatives. They want to read success stories and how they can go about becoming a success story themselves."

I don't agree. I think people who are seriously considering a major step like starting their own business want to have complete information—the risks as well as the rewards. And, in fact, any book that doesn't provide this is doing an injustice to the reader. I'm going to expand this reasoning by devoting most of this chapter to the risks, because the rewards that come with success in small business are almost self-evident.

Most of the risks discussed in this chapter will be familiar to you. But I think it's important to explore each one fully, to understand its implications, to quantify it (if possible), and to estimate its potential impact.

I also want to note here that measures can be taken to minimize, or even eliminate, many risks. The proper business selection, an appropriate startup strategy, and effective management are all important contributions which will help significantly to make a success of your business venture.

LOSS OF A PREDICTABLE INCOME.

Security is what a good job is all about to most people. Sure it's nice if you enjoy the work and the people you associate with, but it's that paycheck that comes every Friday or every 2 weeks or every month that says it all. A paycheck is what makes it possible to stomach the long commute, the hectic pace, the demanding boss, or any of the other complications of the contemporary workaday life.

But a predictable income, that paycheck, more than anything else, is like a giant security blanket. You know (barring unforeseen circumstances) that it's going to be there next week, next month, and next year—to pay the bills that are going to be there next week, next month, and next year.

It takes a special person to give up the financial and emotional security of that regular paycheck. That's why I feel the best way to start a business is on a part-time basis while maintaining employment. In many circumstances this is not possible, however. But there are other ways to wean oneself from a regular paycheck. These are discussed in Chapter 8.

GIVING UP COMPANY-PAID LIFE AND HEALTH INSURANCE.

Most employers provide substantial insurance benefits at little or no cost to the employee. These typically include:

- Life insurance
- Health insurance
- Disability insurance

When you go off on your own, you'll have to find some way to maintain your insurance protection. There are several ways you can do this.

Individual Insurance Protection

Shop around and then purchase protection for yourself and your family. This seems simple enough. And it is. But there are two problems: first, the cost is high, maybe as high as $100 to $150 a month, and second, the protection may not be as good as that offered in a group policy. This is especially true with health insurance. Many individual health insurance plans pay a fixed amount per day for hospitalization. But usually the daily benefit is far below the soaring cost ($100 to $300 a day) of just a hospital room, let alone the additional charges for x-rays, lab tests, and so on.

Group Protection

You can save money and possibly improve coverage by purchasing insurance through some group you belong to or can join. For example, I have maintained my membership in two engineering societies (even though my slide rule has long been retired) because they offer excellent, low-cost life insurance plans. Unfortunately, I haven't been able to find any comprehensive health insurance offered by a group. But, thankfully, our family is covered by Blue Cross/Blue Shield through my wife's job. She's an R.N. and works several days a week at the local hospital. The insurance protection she receives is almost as important as her paycheck.

Company Group Protection

Once your business is in operation, you'll be able to purchase group insurance for your employees. Then you'll be covered by just including yourself in the group. This will still cost you money. But you'll be paying low-cost group rates, and the insurance cost will be a pretax expense.

GIVING UP A RETIREMENT PLAN.

In addition to insurance protection, many employers provide some form of retirement plan. Depending on your age and your years of service with your employer, quitting to run your own business could mean sacrificing sizable retirement benefits. Before you make a decision, you should determine what payments may be due you if you leave.

Then, when you do go off on your own, I thoroughly recommend that you start an Individual Retirement Account (IRA) or a Keogh Retirement Plan. Both allow you to set up tax-sheltered programs to put money aside for your retirement. Actually the IRA plan is available to anyone who does not have a retirement plan. So if you're employed but your company does not have a pension program, you can gain the tax benefits of an IRA.

You can get more information on both the IRA and the Keogh plan from the Internal Revenue Service or from your local library, bank, or savings and loan association.

LOSS OF STATUS SYMBOLS AND PERKS.

Many jobs come with trappings and perquisites that may be difficult to give up. Possibilities include:

- Plush, private office
- Secretary
- Reserved parking space
- Company car
- First-class business travel
- Country club membership

It's unlikely in the early years of your own business that you'll be able to duplicate these creature comforts. Give that some thought if it's important to you.

A more subjective status symbol is being a part of a large, successful company: "Oh, I'm a product manager for General Electric." "I work for IBM." "I'm a line supervisor at the Oldsmobile assembly plant." This type of association, this type of belonging, is important to some people.

But then there are examples of people who apparently have every trapping you could ask for in a job and still chuck it all to go off on their own. John Delorean was a rising star in the executive suite of

General Motors. He had money, position, limousines, corporate airplanes, authority, and responsibility. He had served a successful stint as the general manager of Chevrolet division and was a corporate vice president when he quit. But running his own sports car company offered him more than General Motors could.

LOSS OF SENIORITY.

In a lot of jobs and with a lot of companies, seniority is precious. Union workers and teachers are just two examples of occupations that are steeped in the seniority system. Giving up seniority is a major problem for many people who would like to start their own business. And remember, it's one thing you can't get bck once you give it up.

There is no easy answer to the seniority problem. Archie Bunker gave up his seniority when he bought Kelso's Bar. It worked out all right for him. But his new business was assured success. All his customers were paid actors!

LOSS OF CAREER MOMENTUM.

Loss of career momentum is another risk associated with leaving the world of the employed, but happily its risks are more apparent than real.

The issue here is simply this: How desirable is a job candidate who is seeking employment after an unsuccessful business venture? Will the candidate be looked upon by potential employers as a person who will quit again as soon as another business opportunity arises? Or even worse, will he or she be labeled as a discontent who will sour other workers on the advantages of being an employee?

On the contrary, my observations lead me to believe that the apprehensions concerning the employability of a former small business person are unfounded. Most reenter the job market without any difficulty. Many employers feel that this type of job candidate will contribute experience and knowledge gained in a business venture. This is especially true if one's small business experience is directly related to the position one is applying for.

This brings us to another fascinating point. Many people, after venturing off in a business of their own, change career direction when reentering the job market. The small business experience itself has changed their aspirations and attitudes toward the kind of work they like and the kind of business they want to work in. For these people, career momentum becomes irrelevant.

TEMPORARILY LOWER INCOME.

Temporarily lower income, when starting a business, is not really a risk—it's almost a sure thing. Few new businesses are profitable during their first 6 months or even their first year. And even if they are profitable, only a handful generate enough income to justify a salary for the owner as sizable as he or she was making while employed.

It's critical to recognize this situation and to have enough working capital set aside to cover living expenses during the startup of a business. And this recognition should take into account the fact that even when your business is established enough to support a proprietor's paycheck of a size comparable to the one you used to get as an employee, your *net* spendable income will still be lower.

The reason for this situation is the additional cost associated with being self-employed. There's the health and life insurance that you didn't have to pay for before. And then there's the IRA or Keogh pension plan that you didn't have to pay for before. And finally, there's the good old social security tax. You're taxed at a higher rate as a self-employed person than as an employee. The reason for this is that the employer pays part of the social security tax for each employee. Since you are now your own employer, you have to pay more tax, in total.

You won't equal your employed net spendable income until your self-employed annual income exceeds your employed annual earnings by about $2,000 to $3,000 or more. The bulk of this difference is in pension and insurance expenses.

POSSIBLE LOSS OF PERSONAL ASSETS.

If your business fails, you're going to lose some money. It's as simple as that. And if the money you invest in the business comes from a mortgage on your home or from your savings account, you're obviously risking your personal assets. Or if your business runs up debts that it cannot meet, and you go bankrupt, creditors may attach your personal assets to pay off the obligations.

I know that many books on small business say that you can protect your personal assets by incorporating. That's true in theory. But in reality, when you borrow money, even if you're incorporated, the lender will insist that you sign for the loan, not as a corporate officer, but personally. For example, I know a man who has run a successful retailing business for decades and still his bank insists on his personal signature!

Debt has a way of expanding beyond control in some business ventures. Take the case of Mary Konklin's business, for example.

Several years ago she came up with an idea that appeared to fill a need in the womens' clothing market. She felt that both women who buy ready-to-wear garments and those who make their clothes from patterns have a problem in that the clothes often do not fit properly. Her company was formed to provide parts of garments precut to the proper size, the necessary decorations, and instructions for sewing the garment. All garments were offered in high-quality fabrics.

The business was initially capitalized by a $27,000 bank loan (she already was operating a successful nursery school, so her business credit was established) and a $13,000 loan from her parents.

About a year later the business was alive but not well. Mary borrowed $2,500 from a friend to meet her payroll. She borrowed $10,000 from a local businesswoman and $5,000 from her mother to purchase fabrics.

Six months later, the business was growing rapidly but just barely breaking even, so Mary put her house up as collateral on a $28,000 bank loan. She then said she'd sell her house if she has to in order to raise more capital.

Mary's business, which was originally founded on loans of $40,000, is now is debt for a total of $85,000. And it still isn't making any money!

Many of these kinds of risks can be avoided by sound financial planning, by controlling growth, and by tight control of expenses. For example, since Mary's business was growing rapidly, it might have been better for her to put a damper on expansion by raising her prices significantly. This would have slowed the growth (thereby requiring less capital) and raised the profit on each item sold. Sometimes it is best to turn away business. Especially marginally profitable business.

A POSSIBLE POOR CREDIT RATING.

When a business falls upon hard times, there can be a great impact on the owner's credit rating. This is especially true if the business debt has been secured with personal assets or if the business declares bankruptcy. Beware of finding yourself in this situation! But if you do, seek out professional financial advice. It may save you from disaster.

From a management point of view, serious financial damage can sometimes be avoided by being honest enough with yourself to admit that you're riding a loser. The strategy then becomes a matter of limiting your losses rather than letting pride cloud your judgment.

Quite possibly, the business is failing for reasons beyond your control. An unexpected downturn in the economy, for example, might have decreased consumer spending. Or the city government might have decided to close the street a new store is located on in order to do major repair work. A decrease in traffic during the critical startup period could be disastrous. It's not the storeowner's fault. Should the owner tough it out? Or go out of business to cut losses, and then start over again later? It's a difficult decision. But an open-minded manager will at least consider the possibility. Maybe a special advertising program, focused around a theme of the street being closed ("It's worth the walk to get to . . ."), would improve customer traffic and sales.

REWARDS.

Well, I think I've dispensed enough doom and gloom in this chapter. Let's take a quick look at the rewards that, to many, make all the risks and hard work worthwhile.

I'm going to illustrate this section with a somewhat special story that not only demonstrates beautifully the rewards of self-employment, but also shows that some people who we assume are content with their jobs are, in fact, not at all happy.

Frank Williams received his law degree in night school several years ago. To support his wife and infant daughter he had worked full-time during the day as a shoe salesman. He thought he had it made when he passed the bar examination and got a job with a good law firm. But after 2 years Frank realized that he was not happy. Although the money was good, he resented being told what to do, what to wear, and what cases to work on. As Frank put it, "in a firm, you're just an employee, no matter how much money you make. Your life isn't your own. I made up my mind that I didn't sweat through law school to work for somebody else."

But making it as a solo practitioner isn't easy. Competition is fierce. Law schools are turning out graduates at a record pace. According to the American Bar Association, the lawyer population in the United States has increased to almost 450,000, up about 100,000 in the last 7 years, with another 120,000 students now in law school. And as I noted in Chapter 1, over 70 percent of practicing lawyers work in firms, which are tough competition for an individual lawyer because of their status.

Frank Williams rented an office and waiting room in a modest building for $210 a month. His wife did all his secretarial work in the evenings. Frank hustles for business and always offers his clients that extra portion of personal service. He even wears a pager so his answering service can find him any time during the day. The bulk of his work is in wills and real estate. He takes pride in his work, no matter how small the fee is. "Most lawyers think a real estate closing is small stuff and act like they're doing the client a favor by handling it," says Frank. "But not me. At each closing I've got the papers ready. I'm enthusiastic. The client appreciates it."

Hard work is paying off for Frank Williams. He recently bought a new home in a prestigious suburb and drives a new Cadillac. But Frank has something more important than money—independence and self-satisfaction. "I see some of my classmates getting lost in big firms, and I'm glad that I'm not them. I get a kick out of seeing *my* name on the door."

Simply stated, the rewards for making it in your own business are these:

- Significant income
- Maybe even an extraordinary income
- Entrepreneur status
- A sense of accomplishment
- Freedom and independence
- Enjoyable work
- Pride

Let's examine each of these rewards in more detail.

Income   One of the most pleasing aspects of income from a small business is that it is not limited by arbitrary forces. As a small business person, one's income is limited only by one's ability to succeed and expand. There's no waiting to be promoted,, or hoping for a big increase in the next contract. A recent Harris survey of small business owners in New York determined that they have an average income of $106,700!

Of course, there is a great variability in the earnings potential of different types of businesses. And this variability can put a ceiling on how much one can make. So it's critical to select a type of business that has an earnings potential high enough to satisfy your desires.

Depending on your aspirations, it's possible that not even a "gold mine" like a McDonald's fast-food outlet will generate enough income. Currently, a McDonald's restaurant generates an average net income of about $70,000 to $90,000 per year on revenues of about $650,000 to $950,000. And this is extremely high for franchises in general. The average net income of all the franchised business in the United States is probably below $50,000.

Later on in this book I'll show you how to get a good handle on the income potential of the businesses you're interested in. I'll also show you how to sort out the important aspects of net income— owner's salary, net profit, and return on investment.

Entrepreneur status A special status comes with being a business owner. Friends, relations, and acquaintances respect and some even secretly envy entrepreneurs. In a sense, this status is akin to the status given to American pioneers who trekked across miles of desolation to carve a homestead and a livelihood out of the wilderness. Creators of new businesses are, in fact, the pioneers of our free enterprise system.

A sense of accomplishment Taking the American pioneer analogy one step further, I'm sure our forebears felt a great sense of accomplishment. I don't think it's an exaggeration to say that small business owners feel the same way. And they deserve to. A person who takes a run-down old Victorian house and turns it into a thriving restaurant and gift shop has accomplished a great deal. As a matter of fact, every business owner is an achiever and knows the satisfaction that comes with "doing it my way."

How often have you made an important contribution as an employee, only to have your boss, or your bosses' boss, get the credit and the glory? This can't happen when you own your own business.

Freedom and independence I know a woman who was the supervisor of a large clerical operation at a division of a Fortune 500 corporation. She pushed for several years to update and streamline operations, in part by taking advantage of word-processing equipment. Management repeatedly balked at her proposals. Frustration with her lack of freedom and independence finally became too much. She quit to start her own automated secretarial service. Her husband and teenage children rallied behind her. Now, just one year later, her new business is thriving, and she has the autonomy to make the decisions she feels are proper. The correctness of her judgments is born out by the fact that her former employer is now one of her largest customers! They give her their rush jobs because she can do their work faster and more accurately than they can.

Enjoyable work   All of us want to gain as much enjoyment from our work as possible. The work we do consumes more of our waking hours than any other activity, so why shouldn't it contribute to our happiness instead of making us miserable? The key to finding enjoyable work in a business of your own is careful self-examination and a methodical analysis of alternatives. Too often, people choose a business just based on income potential. But work content is also important. More on this in later chapters.

Pride   Self-employed people and small business owners are a proud lot. One of the most striking aspects of this pride focuses on a self-awareness that they're making it on their own. They feel good about themselves because they know they aren't beholden to anyone or any company for a job. Self-employed people and small business owners take a special pride in knowing that they're succeeding despite the hurdles, despite the gloom mongers, despite government regulations. They know it can be done because they've done it. They're proud of it, and rightly so.

THREE

Why businesses fail . . . and why businesses succeed.

This is possibly the first book about small businesses to deal honestly and frankly with the topic of small business failure.

Let's face it, failure is a fact of life. But being aware of the mistakes and miscalculations of others can be instructive. It may help you to avoid them if you decide to start a business.

Examining the causes of small business failures is not unlike a defensive-driving course. Knowing what can go wrong and learning how to minimize the risks make people who have taken this type of course better and safer drivers. Obviously, the way to avoid all risks from automobile accidents is never to get into a car and never to walk near a street. And the only way to totally avoid the possibility of small business failure is never to get involved in one. But, as we all know, risk is a part of living. Thinking people realize this and do what they can, not to avoid risk, but to minimize it through knowledge and understanding.

DECIPHERING THE FAILURE STATISTICS.

The most widely publicized and probably the most reliable data on small business failure are published annually by Dun & Bradstreet, Inc., in *The Business Failure Record*. Although it isn't specifically limited to failures of *small* businesses, it primarily documents small business failures because 9 out of 10 businesses in this country are small. Besides, probably the failure rate is higher for small businesses than for large businesses. (Often large companies are acquired as "attractive turnaround situations" before they get close to bankruptcy.)

The *Failure Record* tabulates failures in five types of businesses:

- Manufacturing
- Wholesaling
- Retailing
- Construction
- Commercial services

It's interesting that the *underlying cause* of failure, as Dun & Bradstreet puts it, does not vary significantly from one type of business to another. So we can look at the *total* failure figures as representative of *each* of the five business types. Before proceeding I want to mention that Dun & Bradstreet defines a business failure as a business that is involved in court proceedings or voluntary actions concerning loss to creditors. If a business is liquidated voluntarily, and creditors are paid in full, this is not tallied as a failure. Obviously, this narrow definition makes the data less useful.

According to Dun & Bradstreet, the *underlying cause* of business failure are:

Underlying cause	Share of failures,%
Incompetence	42.3
Unbalanced experience	23.0
Lack of experience in the line	13.8
Lack of managerial experience	13.0
Neglect	0.8
Disaster	0.8
Fraud	0.5
Unknown	5.8
Total	100.0

As you can see, incompetence and several forms of experience deficiencies account for over 90 percent of the failures. The problem with this data is that it's not very enlightening. All it says is that incompetent people and people with experience deficiencies are likely to fail in business. Not earthshaking news.

In an attempt to improve the usefulness of the data, the *Failure Record* also distributes failure by *apparent cause*. Here's that tabulation:

Apparent cause	Share of failures, %
Inadequate sales	49.9*
Competitive weakness	25.3
Heavy operating expenses	13.0
Receivables difficulties	8.3
Inventory difficulties	7.7
Excessive fixed assets	3.2
Poor location	2.7
Neglect	0.8
Disaster	0.8
Fraud	0.5
Other	1.1

*Numbers do not add to 100 percent because some failures are attributed to a combination of apparent causes.

These numbers are more informative than the others. They tell us, for example, that:

- About half of all businesses in the Dun & Bradstreet sample failed because of inadequate sales. I buy that. A weak marketing effort is often fatal.

- Competitive weaknesses, which may also be interpreted as poor marketing, caused 25.3 percent of failures.

- Next down the column is a group of four apparent causes (operating expenses, receivables, inventory, and fixed assets) that total about 32 percent. All these are interrelated problems involving internal operations.

• The only other significant percentage is poor location (2.7 percent). Incidentally, this varies from as high as 5.3 percent for retailing to as low as about 0.5 percent for construction and manufacturing. Location again is a marketing (i.e., inadequate sales because of location) problem.

This all boils down to two broad categories that are the apparent causes of almost all business failures in the sample.

1. Marketing or sales difficulties (77.9 percent)
    •Inadequate sales (49.9 percent)
    •Competitive weaknesses (25.3 percent)
    •Poor location (2.7 percent)
2. Internal operating difficulties (32.2 percent)
    •Heavy operating expenses (13.0 percent)
    •Receivables difficulties (8.3 percent)
    •Inventory difficulties (7.7 percent)
    •Excessive fixed assets (3.2 percent)

I think that now we're finally learning something from the numbers. First, we're learning that people can't succeed in any business if they don't sell enough of whatever they're selling. Basic, isn't it? But how many people start businesses without doing what is necessary to assure that they are going to satisfy a customer's needs or wants at a profitable price. Second, we're learning that people need more than the ability to sell a product or service successfully. People need some management competence to properly handle a small business's internal affairs (such as collecting receivables and controlling operating expenses).

All in all, the *Failure Record* is telling us that to succeed in a business, people must produce a product or service efficiently and must find sufficient customers who want to buy it. So simple, yet often so difficult to accomplish.

In the remainder of this chapter we're going to explore further some of the important *specific* causes of small business failures. Effectively avoiding situations that can lead to failure will go a long way toward contributing to your success in a small business. Much of the following comes from my experience as a business consultant and from discussions with numerous persons who run small businesses.

MARKETING THAT UNTRIED NEW IDEA.

Everybody, at least once in their lifetime, has an idea for a fantastic new product or service. A few of these ideas make their creators into millionaires. The stories of McDonald's, The Pet Rock, and Colonel Sander's Kentucky Fried Chicken are almost folk legends.

I have enough experience with human judgment to know that most people recognize that fantastic success based on an untried idea is a one-in-a-million happening. So I get upset when I read articles and books that insist that the way to succeed in a small business is to commercialize your untried idea. Our instincts tell us that this is very risky. But, unfortunately, budding entrepreneurs all too often believe what they see in black and white, rather than what they feel.

I just read a very dignified book about small business, for example, published by a highly respected company, professing that the *only* way to ensure small business success is to venture into uncharted waters. This book characterizes "me-too-ism" as the road to disaster.

There is also a class of books that are devoted to patenting new-product ideas and, therefore, tout the virtues of newness. They contain useful information, but their single-minded emphasis on newness as the route to success is erroneous and potentially damaging.

To show you what I mean, let's look at two facts.

Fact 1 All evidence clearly shows that the surest way to succeed in a small business is to purchase a franchise from an established company. Some of these companies have failure rates for new franchises of less than 10 percent. But isn't franchising the ultimate in me-too-ism? It's taking someone else's success and duplicating it in new locations.

Fact 2   Giant multimillion dollar Fortune 500 companies have difficulty succeeding with untried new products and services (see Appendix). Surveys show that over half of all new consumer products introduced by established, profitable, big companies fail! If these well-funded, sophisticated companies, with their research laboratories and their elaborate marketing research techniques, fail more often than not, what chance do people like us have with our new idea? Slim at best, I say.

Logic suggests that the way to succeed in a business is to utilize a proven success formula. There are several ways to do this:

1.   Duplicate in location B the successful business operating in location A.

2.   Purchase a successful, ongoing business.

3.   Differentiate a new business by slightly modifying a proven success formula.

4.   Buy a franchise.

There will be more on these concepts later. I just wanted to introduce some of them here, so I don't leave the impression that small business success is beyond your reach.

LACK OF MARKETING ORIENTATION.

A second specific reason for business failure is lack of market orientation. Here's an illustration that demonstrates this pitfall beautifully.

Two scientists who were working at a private research facility discovered a new process for generating ultraviolet light. They figured that this new lamp would be more efficient and longer-lasting than existing devices. It also had the advantage that it could be activated almost instantly. A partnership was formed, and with $12,000 in savings, a business was begun on a part-time basis. Several years of research and development and about $60,000 later, the partners had a product. But in all this time, they gave little or no thought to who was going to buy the new lamp. They had a vague idea that ultraviolet lamps were needed to make certain industrial chemicals and needed by doctors to treat some skin disorders, but that was all.

When marketing efforts were finally begun, they were ill conceived and misdirected. Letters were sent to industrial chemical producers. There was no response. Any person experienced in industrial sales could have predicted that. Sophisticated industrial products are not sold by mail! Next, an ad was placed in a trade journal. No response. Again, not surprising. Finally, one of the partners began calling on industrial chemical producers that used conventional ultraviolet lamps. He discovered that the advantages of their new process were not needed in industrial chemical processing.

At this point, the new company, by all rights, deserved to fail. They were doing things backwards. You don't design a product and then find a market; you should find a need and then design a product to meet it.

But lady luck was watching over the ultraviolet lamp venturers. While on vacation, one of the partners decided to call on a company that printed packaging materials. They just happened to be working on a new printing process that required inexpensive ultraviolet light for drying the ink. Lightning struck. Their lamps were tested and a $400,000 order was placed within 2 months! With the luck these two had, they should spend more time in Las Vegas and less time in the laboratory.

However, all too often, lady luck isn't there. So companies that are founded without an emphasis on proper marketing are almost sure to fail. Technology-oriented companies are the most likely to fall into this trap, but all types of new small businesses are vulnerable. New retailers open their doors without any plans for advertising or promotion. Machine shops lease space and buy machines without determining if a market need exists. Contractors go into business without sizing up their competition.

In an oversimplified sense, marketing is business. Not to recognize this is to ask for failure. To emphasize this point, and to drive home the need for small business marketing, I've devoted all the last chapter of this book to selling. If you're serious about succeeding in a business of your own, don't stop until you have read Chapter 15.

POOR LOCATION.

Location is extremely important in all retailing and in restaurants. The Dun & Bradstreet *Business Failure Record* lists location as the apparent cause of failure for 5 percent of retailers. This sounds low and it may well be. But even if location causes only 5 percent of the failures, a better location would probably transform many marginally successful retailers into prosperous ones.

A friend of mine, who has years of experience in retailing, knows the value of good location. He is currently diversifying into a fast-food operation. He found a prime location 6 months before his restaurant could open. But he didn't let that deter him from signing a lease. He'd rather pay rent on an empty storefront in a good location for 6 months than take the chance of being stuck forever with a less desirable location.

One mistake some people make is to rent a store in a location that has a history of failure. For some unexplained reason they feel they'll be able to turn the situation around. Unless you have strong evidence suggesting that location wasn't the cause of the previous tenants' "going-out-of-business" sale, pass up these bargain rent deals.

Of course, successful franchising companies have turned site location into a science. Demographics, traffic density, sign visibility, competitor's proximity, and other variables all play an important role in their selection criteria. More on site selection in Chapter 4.

GOING WITH A LOSER.

Some people buy or start businesses that have a very slim chance of succeeding. A typical example is a small houseplant shop that was started recently in my town. It was located in a busy shopping area in an attractive building. But, also in that same shopping area, within a block, was some tough competition. Down the street was the community's leading florist, so successful and so well known that, to local people, its name was almost synonymous with flowers. It didn't carry many potted plants, but it had a decent assortment.

A block away was a major food store. It had an apparently thriving houseplant department that offered everything from cactus to jade plants. And on top of all this local competition, the largest florist/ nursery in the metropolitan area had a major outlet about 5 miles away. The woman who opened the new plant shop acknowledged the competition but was blind to its possible impact on her. She said, "I'm offering friendly, personal service and high-quality plants. Plus, I give all kinds of free advice. What exposure is right for what plant. How frequently to water and fertilize. None of these other places do that, do they?" No they don't. At least not very often. But they have other things going for them such as:

- Low prices and convenience in the food store
- A great reputation for quality in the local florist
- TV advertising and an amazing variety (pitched as "every bloomin' thing") at the major florist/nursery

I'd say that the new houseplant shop was a failure before it opened its doors. It lasted less than 5 months.

Earlier I noted that franchises are a relatively safe form of new business venture. But there are losers in franchises, too. For example:

- A fellow I know spent $10,000 for a computer bookkeeping franchise. He lost the $10,000 when the franchise went bankrupt several months after he bought in.
- A large, well-known, franchised fried chicken chain recently declared bankruptcy. New franchisees were joining this outwardly successful operation right up to the time the news of bankruptcy hit the financial pages. Chapter 5 tells how to avoid this pitfall.

To complete this scenario I should also point out that there are losers to be found when purchasing ongoing businesses. New start-ups and franchises aren't the only guilty parties. Analyzing the opportunities associated with the purchase of an ongoing business takes care and understanding. See Chapter 6.

INADEQUATE CAPITAL.

Most owners of successful small businesses feel that the prime cause of small business failure is inadequate capital. They know how important sufficient capital resources are, and they know how difficult it is to raise additional capital to carry a business through the initial lean period. There are three common ways a new business gets into a capital-short situation:

First, naïvely underestimating the capital needed to get off to a good start. This is a common shortcoming, but there is no excuse for it. Numerous resources are available to assist you in making sound judgments (e.g., SBA publications, Bank of America's *Small Business Reporter* publications, experienced small business owners, and accountants).

Second, some people put their heads in a cloud and start businesses with less capital than they estimated they needed. This is sheer lunacy. It's far better to delay the start until you've saved enough or borrowed from friends. Do anything, but get what you need before you start.

Third, expanding rapidly sucks up sorely needed working capital. It's quite easy to expand yourself right *out* of business.

It's sad but true. Too often businesses that have a good chance of making it fail because of liquidity problems. This simply means that the business doesn't have the cash to pay its bills when they come due. You may have thousands of dollars in accounts receivable, but if you don't have money to meet the payroll or to pay suppliers, you're in big trouble. Any one of the three common mistakes I described above can get you into this predicament.

LACK OF PROPER EXPERIENCE.

Data presented earlier in this chapter suggest that unbalanced experience, lack of experience in the line, and lack of management experience account for about half of the business failures in the sample. This may be a little high, but there is no question that lack of experience contributes to many small business failures.

But there are ways to make up for experience deficiencies:

- Work for someone in the kind of business you want to start. This can often be done on a part-time basis (evenings, weekends).
- Take on a partner with the needed experience.
- Hire outside professional experience (accountants, collection services, advertising experts, etc.).

It's also encouraging to note that experience is not always desirable. Quite a few franchisers *prefer* franchisees who have no experience in their businesses. These franchisers have found that experienced people have preconceived notions and biases that conflict with the way the franchisee is "supposed" to operate his or her business.

THERE'S LIGHT AT THE END OF THE TUNNEL.

I don't want to end this chapter with the impression that the causes of business failures are insurmountable. On the contrary, they can be overcome with proper knowledge and diligence. The rest of this book provides valuable information and insights that can assist the conscientious new small business owner to avoid failure-causing pitfalls.

FOUR

The lowdown on your business choice.

The variety of small business opportunities is almost limitless. However, there are six business categories which, taken together, account for the vast majority of small business startups and small business purchases:

- Mail order
- Retailing
- Restaurants
- Manufacturing
- Service businesses
- New product or service ideas

It's quite likely that the business you're thinking of starting, and even several alternative businesses which appeal to you, fall into these six classifications. In this chapter, we're going to examine the myths and realities for each of these business types.

MAIL ORDER—PLUSES AND MINUSES.

One of the single most successful mail-order products has to be books explaining how easy it is to succeed in the mail-order business!

Some of these books are openly marketed as mail-order success books, while others are promoted as books that reveal ("for the first time") a secret yet simple way to make a *bundle*. When these books arrive, the buyer discovers that mail order is the "secret."

Please don't misunderstand. I don't want to give the impression that I'm totally down on mail order as a business opportunity. That's not the case. It's just that I want to make it clear from the start that mail order is not an easy road to riches—unless that is, you can successfully market some version of the mail-order success book!

Its Many Appeals

Mail order (direct marketing, or direct response, if you prefer more sophisticated titles) has many appeals to people interested in a business of their own, such as:

- *Low investment* A mail-order business can realistically be started for as little as $1,500.
- *At home* A modest scale mail-order business can be operated from the home.
- *Part-time* One can maintain the security of regular employment while starting a mail-order business.
- *Little specialized knowledge* Theoretically, all one needs is a product, and an ad (or a brochure and a mailing list) to get into business.

Add to these advantages the chance to realize the dream of having hundreds or even thousands of orders flowing in each day, and it's easy to see why mail order is the stuff that best-selling books are made of.

And success, fantastic success in mail order is possible. I know of a mail-order company that has been making well over $100,000 in owner salary and net profit from the sale of a single product for over 15 years. The only advertising they do is a monthly half-page spot in a national magazine. A modest manufacturing set-up cranks out each product (personalized with the customer's name) and packages it for shipping. The average order size is about $10. It's just a beautiful little business. No hassles. Few, if any, customer complaints or returns. And it was started by a man with no marketing or mail-order experience. He was making a profit after 2 months and has made a profit every month since then. This business is the epitome of the mail-order fantasy. And there are hundreds of other ones cited in mail-order books. Many may be exaggerated, but no doubt most are based on factual case histories.

But there has to be some problems with the mail-order business. Or else, by now, all of our friends and relatives would be running lucrative businesses out of their garages or basements!

Most Space Ads Don't Pay

A space ad is the typical mail-order ad you see in the home shopper's section of magazines like *Better Homes and Gardens.* It usually has a photo of the product, a headline, a brief description, a price, and information for ordering.

What I mean by "don't pay" is that most space ads don't generate enough orders to make them profitable. Here's an illustration. A one-time ad in a national magazine might cost $1,000. The product in the ad is priced at $3. On the average, this ad will generate orders of from $500 to $1,500. With $500 in orders the mail-order company is in a deep loss situation.

And even with $1,500 in orders, it's a losing proposition. Here's why. The product cost (including the product itself, packaging, and mailing) is probably about $1, or one-third of the selling price. The $1,500 in orders represents 500 units at $1 each. So total product cost to fill the orders is $500. Add this to the $1,000 ad cost and you can see that the $1,500 in orders just covers advertising and product costs. There is nothing to cover overhead and there is nothing left for the owner's pocket.

"Then if space ads don't make money, why do mail-order companies keep placing them in magazines?" you ask. Because the primary purpose of space ads is not to make money. Its purpose is to get names of mail-order buyers to add to the mailing list.

You see, *most* mail order companies make their money by mailing a catalog to a list of names. Now, all of a sudden, that simple spare-time, basement business gets inordinately more complicated. Instead of placing an ad each month, you must send a catalog 2 or 3 or 4 times a year to 10,000 or 20,000 or 100,000 names. Instead of having just one product, you have a catalog and warehouse shelves full of literally dozens or even hundreds of products. And instead of preparing one ad, you must prepare an entire catalog. I knew one couple who went this route; their "catalog", while it was in progress, was spread out all over their living room floor for weeks.

While we're on the subject of catalogs, there is one other harsh reality. It is that catalogs are not necessarily gold mines, either. The first catalogs produced by new mail-order companies hardly ever make money. A loss of several thousand dollars is more typical. Eventually, catalogs do pay, but it usually takes time and patience.

Copycats Can Kill You

Say you get lucky and hit upon a product that does extremely well when promoted in space ads in magazines. In fact, suppose it does so well it produces a handsome profit. Is your basement mail-order business out of the woods? I'm afraid not.

There is still the copycat to contend with. Copycats watch space ads to see which ones are repeated frequently. They are also "wired in" with advertising agencies that specialize in mail-order advertising and with magazine space salespeople. Through observation and all these connections, copycats know when a product is doing well. And as the name implies, they copy it—maybe in a little different size, a little different color, a little different price. But it can cut into the original product's sales deeply.

Happily, there are several ways to guard against copycats. The patent is the most obvious, but, as I point out in Chapter 7, this doesn't always work. The surest protection is a prohibitively high cost of entry. Say, for example, the tooling needed to make your product costs $20,000. Most copycats, who are typically small-time operators, wouldn't risk this much money to enter someone else's business.

The copyright is another good protection against copycats. This is why coprighted mail-order books are such good mail-order items. At one point in my own small business career, I seriously considered the possibility of publishing my own books and selling them by mail order. The copyright protection was one of the primary factors that attracted me. Unfortunately, very few viable mail-order products lend themselves to copyright.

Consider the Competition

The Direct Mail/Marketing Association estimates that over $90 billion worth of goods and services are sold each year using direct response techniques. It's a massive market, but this means that there is much competition. And the competition isn't just coming from other people operating out of *their* basements. The competition is Sears, Ward's, Spiegel, Fingerhut, American Express, and others—along with hundreds of small companies.

Look at the competition from the consumer's point of view. Every consumer, including you, is bombarded with direct advertising messages. They come in the mailbox (gadget catalogs, fruitcake, or frozen meat catalogs). They come on TV and on the radio. The announcer pleads with us to call an 800 number to get three albums—"The Best of Julius LaRosa for $9.95." Or he might entreat us to order a new kitchen tool that will slice or dice a bushel of potatoes in 3 minutes.

All kidding aside, the competition for the consumer's direct-response dollar is fierce. If you are seriously considering the mail-order business, don't overlook this reality. And don't fail to plan a strategy to combat it.

I suggest the target market-segment approach. It involves concentrating on the select group of customers who will be most receptive to your advertising and your products. If your product is a widget, then ask:

- What type of consumer is most likely to buy a widget?
- Is there a cost-effective response approach by which I can reach these people?
- Is the market potential big enough to build a business around my product, or a catalog of related products?

While we're on the topic of reaching customers, I want to make two other points. (1) There is another effective way to reach customers, besides space ads and catalogs. It's the plain old-fashioned letter. It's used every day and it works well for certain products. You can find out more about this approach from mail-order books or from experienced mail-order people. (2) The best mailing list for a business is probably the one it develops from space ads, direct-mail campaigns, and catalog mailings. However, you can also "rent" all kinds of mailing lists. The cost is about $15 to $40 per 1000 names and addresses. List rental is one reason why you and I get so many offers in the mail from companies we never heard of. They probably rented a list that included your name and address.

Two Approaches

Based on what I've written so far on mail-order business opportunities, you've probably gathered that I'm not overly enthusiastic about the "catalog" approach to mail-order success. This is a personal bias of mine. But don't let it unduly influence you. Developing a mailing list and catalog from space advertising is a viable business strategy. But it takes a person who is so inclined.

The other approach to mail-order success is to focus on a single (hopefully copycat-proof) product. It can be marketed either through space advertising or by direct mail campaigns, whichever is more appropriate. A combination might even be right.

One thought to keep in mind: Remember that if you follow the single-product approach, mail order is nothing more than a method of distribution. If mail order is not the best distribution method for your particular product, then forget mail order. Your goal is to maximize your profit, not to see how many orders you can produce in the mail. A more appropriate distribution route might be to sell to distributors or even directly to retailers. Mail order in this situation is a tool; one that may or may not work. If it doesn't work, get out of the mail-order *distribution* mode, and sell your product some other way.

Pricing and Advertising Expenses

Margins in mail order are high. If you expect to succeed in this business *your* margins must be high. Experienced mail-order people mark up their products by at least a factor of three. For example, an item costing $2 (including packaging and postage) should sell for at least $6. Hopefully, the market will be able to support an even higher price. Say $8 or $10 or even $15.

Prepare to spend about 50 percent of your sales dollar for advertising. This could be space ads, direct mail, TV, radio, or whatever. But just expect to spend 30, 40, or 50 cents to create $1 in sales. This is why you need such a high mark-up. An item costing $2 that you sell for $10 may require $5 in advertising. This leaves you with a gross margin of $3 ($10– $2– $5).

RETAILING—THE MOST POPULAR.

More people who are starting or purchasing a business enter retailing than any other category. About two out of five new business startups are in the retailing portion of our economy. This is only logical, I guess, since retailing is the largest single sector of our diverse business community.

People are typically drawn to retailing as a business opportunity for two reasons: (1) we are all familiar with it; and (2) operating a retailing business appears relatively uncomplicated.

Retailing Outlook

Personally, I'm pleased that many people choose retailing as *their* business opportunity. I say this because I'm convinced that retailing provides a solid, viable route to successful self-employment; a straightforward route that doesn't depend on being exceptional or having an exceptional business concept. I feel that anyone with average talents who enters a healthy, prospering facet of retailing, in a good location, with conscientious management and hard work, can make a go of it. This sounds almost too easy, but in reality it's not. So I want to repeat it, in slightly different form, for emphasis. Retailing success requires:

- Getting into a viable retailing category
- Providing sound management skills and judgment
- Being conscientious and diligent

Here's an example of what I mean. Located in a trendy new shopping center was a T-shirt store. Its business was selling T-shirts monogrammed with transfers selected by the customer and applied to the right size and color T-shirt, while the customer watches. You've probably seen these types of operations. For unknown reasons, this particular store was not doing well. Daily sales were as low as $25. Gross sales for each of the first 2 years of operation were about $50,000.

The owner decided to sell. And two young maintenance men, who happened to work in the shopping center, decided to buy. They paid $10,000 for the T-shirt business. Their wives encouraged the venture and offered to help staff the store. None of the four knew anything about T-shirts or retailing.

The seller explained the business to the buyers and told them where to buy shirts and transfers. But before taking any of her advice, the four of them visited other T-shirt stores. They looked at store layout, T-shirt quality and selection, transfer selection, and shirt manufacturer names.

After this informal "market research," the four young business people made some changes. First, they upgraded the quality of the shirts from "cheapest" to "good" quality cotton-polyester blends. Next, they broadened the lines of shirts, almost tripling selection and inventory, and added sweatshirts. Transfer selection was also expanded and modified to appeal to a broader cross section of consumers.

To top off the transition the store's name was also changed to give a fresh image. One thing wasn't changed, however—the prices. The new owners' research told them that prices were high enough. They were hoping that superior merchandise and an aggressive advertising campaign would substantially boost volume.

You know what? That's just what happened! Sales skyrocketed. Annual gross went from $50,000 to $250,000! This created internal management problems, of course. At first, the store was always running out of fast-moving items. This necessitated wasteful, time-consuming emergency trips to suppliers and distributors. Also, extra part-time help was added to cover peak demand periods.

Another interesting aspect. Neither of our maintenance men have given up their jobs in the shopping center. The business is run as a two-family operation. Everyone pitches in on the sales side. One partner does the books, and his wife selects and orders the T-shirt transfers. The other partner orders the T-shirts, and his wife does billing and miscellaneous secretarial chores.

This success story illustrates perfectly what I'm trying to say in this section:

- Success in retailing doesn't depend on being exceptional or having an exceptional business concept.
- Success does depend on being in a viable, solid business, in a good location—but this is not enough.
- Good judgment, effective management, and hard work are required to bring the enterprise up to its fullest potential.

The Right Type of Retailing

While promoting an earlier small business book, I made appearances on several radio talk shows, the kind where listeners call in to ask questions or express opinions. I did shows in Chicago, Dallas, Providence, Toledo, etc. And one of the most frequently asked questions was, "Ken, what business do you recommend I start?" Another version of the same basic question was "Which will be the fastest growing and most profitable businesses in the years ahead?"

These questions raised several problems for me. I can't possibly tell someone else what they should do. The person who is going to live with a business day in and day out must choose it. Also, a business opportunity shouldn't be chosen just on the basis of profit and growth. Thought must be given to its impact on your desired lifestyle, the types of work you enjoy, how much time you're willing to devote, and so on. I cannot predict the future. I don't have ESP.

But what I can do for you is to emphasize the importance of picking a type of retailing that has a *proven track record* of success, with no foreseeable changes on the horizon to inhibit that success.

Let's go back to T-shirt stores. Conversations with two or three owners of T-shirt stores would convince anyone that this is a thriving retailing category. T-shirts are in, especially T-shirts with pictures and words on them. Visiting T-shirt stores in various parts of town and just observing store traffic and watching the sales being rung up should tell us something positive.

But, the future for T-shirt stores is more nebulous. If you want to get into a business that you're pretty sure will be around and prospering 10 or 12 years from now, I wouldn't choose a T-shirt store. I wouldn't hesitate to choose a convenience grocery store or a florist, though. Then again, if you want a lucrative, fast-paced business that's a little more "loose and relaxed," and you don't mind an uncertain future, maybe T-shirts are for you.

There are hundreds of different types of retailing opportunities. I could make a list of those that I think are winners and those that I think are losers. But that wouldn't serve your needs. I don't have the time or the desire to investigate these properly. But you do. Look for a type of business that:

1.   You feel good about
2.   Has a proven record of success
3.   Has a future outlook that fits your needs and personality

Remember, many different types of retailing operations have proven records of success. So, if you think a retailing business is for you, pick out one that you like, and forge ahead.

Location

Selecting the site for a new retailing enterprise is extremely important. In fact, it is deemed so important by franchising companies, that some have spent tens of thousands of dollars developing site selection criteria for new franchises. And they put a good deal of effort into each new location decision.

If you're *buying* an ongoing retailing business, location should also be important to you. Who's to say that the person who originally started the business made a wise choice? If you decide to buy the business, you're probably locked into its location. But, if the site doesn't measure up, you may rightly decide not to invest.

Site selection can be as sophisticated or as basic as you want to make it. The key to successful site selection is to understand what makes a successful location for the particular retailing activity you're interested in. A successful location for a hardware store may not necessarily be a successful location for a toy store. So just picking a location in a thriving mall or business district is not enough.

The best way to start is to analyze several successful existing locations of businesses like your chosen one. Then, when you find out *why* they are good locations, you can duplicate those characteristics in your own site selection. Of if you're buying an ongoing business, you can compare the characteristics of the successful locations to those of the one you're considering.

Specifically, a successful location depends on these four variables:

1. Nature of the population in the market area
2. Income level in the area
3. Convenience and visibility
4. Competition in the area

Let's examine each of these in detail:

Population The number of potential customers within a market area should be estimated as accurately as possible. Federal census data are probably the most reliable resource. However, note that you may be better off counting something besides total population. Maybe your market will be young singles. So try to estimate this instead. Are there large apartment complexes in the neighborhood? That's a good sign. Or suppose your retailing operation's potential depends upon the number of automobiles in the area. Then get information on automobile registrations.

When looking at population, you should always consider trends. Nothing is unchanging. Population characteristics change. Look at 10-year historical trends and projections, if available, for things like average family size, distribution of age groups, etc.

Income Does the success of your store depend on attracting a large number of well-to-do heads of households? If so, you'd better locate conveniently near them. The 10-year census reports the income of 20 percent of the total population on a national, state, county, city, and census tract basis. Other sources of income data include local planning commissions, employment offices, newspapers, banks, and savings and loans. The type of income may also be important. Is your business dependent on family income, disposable income, or what?

Convenience and visibility Convenience means ease of parking or location near a major interchange, among other things. Visibility may or may not be important. But surely some visibility is desirable. If zoning permits, you can enhance visibility with signs. Some franchised retail outlets require a site to have a sign visible from the main highway for a given number of seconds at the posted speed limit. This may or may not be cutting it too fine for your purpose.

The number of people, either on foot or in cars, that pass an establishment per hour can be critically important to its success. This may be especially critical for impulse-related retailers like candy shops. But for some retailing operations, traffic density is meaningless. If you are convenient and consumers can find you easily, that's all that really counts.

Competition   Earlier I mentioned a defunct plant shop that located within 3 blocks of both a long-established, well-known florist and a thriving plant department in a supermarket. *That* business in *that* location was just asking to be buried by competition. A famous business dictum is "Know your competition." Heeding this advice begins by knowing *where* they are. A given population and income level can only support so much of a given type of business. So look for an area that is not being adequately supplied or one that is growing rapidly.

Many retailers, both new and established, are in a quandary over the desirability of locating in a shopping center, compared to an established traditional business district. Rents are typically higher in a mall, but traffic is higher also. But mall hours are longer, so operating there might cut more deeply into your personal life. For some businesses there really is no choice. But if yours is one that has succeeded in both environments, consider all the ramifications, then do what seems best for you.

Initial Investment Requirements

As the old saying goes, "It takes money to make money." This is certainly true in retailing. The amount of initial investment capital needed varies greatly depending upon:

- Type of retailing
- Store square footage
- Store location
- Geographical area

What this says is that nobody writing a book can tell you how much money you'll need to get started. You're going to have to determine that yourself. But there are some helpful tools. The SBA has aids for establishing startup expenses. The problem with these is that they are primarily fill-in-the-blank type forms. These forms will make sure you consider most expense factors, but they provide little assistance in judging actual dollar amounts.

Also, the *Small Business Reporter,* published by the Bank of America, has at least half-a-dozen booklets, each dealing with a particular type of retailing. And each gives a breakdown in dollars for fixtures and equipment, opening costs and initial operating expenses. These are a good start, if one happens to exist in the retailing segment that you're going into. But these, too, have their weaknesses. Some are 4, 5, or 6 years old. Inflation has taken its toll on the validity of the figures. Also, as the publication correctly points out, all the figures are estimates for a typical operation. In reality, probably no store is typical.

Despite the shortcomings of published figures, I think it's valuable to present some data here. These will give you some idea of the range and magnitude of initial investment required. I have adjusted all the figures for inflation, so all are comparable at current cost levels (Table 1).

You should develop your own initial investment requirement figures. Make sure you include all the following items:

Opening Costs
- Lease deposits
- Licenses and taxes
- Insurance
- Professional services (legal and accounting)
- Fixtures and equipment
- Leasehold improvements
- Security system
- Inventory investment
- Miscellaneous

Operating Costs
- Rent
- Advertising and promotion
- Utilities and telephone
- Supplies

Table 1 Capital Investment Requirements

Retail Type	Size		Opening costs	3-month operating costs	Total
	Gross sales	Square footage			
Hobby/craft	$200,000	2000	$25,000–$40,000	$12,000–$18,000	$37,000–$ 58,000
Toy	300,000	3000	45,000– 75,000	20,000– 30,000	65,000– 105,000
Apparel	250,000	2000	40,000– 70,000	10,000– 15,000	50,000– 85,000
Shoe	150,000	1500	50,000– 60,000	10,000– 15,000	60,000– 75,000
Consumer electronics	400,000	2000	55,000– 90,000	25,000– 40,000	80,000– 130,000

- Wages (for owner and employees)
- Professional services
- Cash reserve

Note that the wages item, above, includes owner's salary. Most people who have started successful businesses stress the importance of paying oneself a regular salary, right from the start. It doesn't have to be a "fair market" salary, but it should be at least on a substantive level. New owners who don't do this fall into the trap of drawing money out of the business when they need it or whenever they feel the business can afford it. This practice has frequently ended up entirely disrupting the sound financial management of the business.

The best source of information to help you estimate opening and operating expense levels is people with experience in your particular facet of retailing. People to contact include accountants, business brokers, merchandise suppliers, and, of course, retail store owners. If your business does not pose a threat to theirs, most will be happy to share their experience and expertise with you.

It never fails to amaze me how knowledgeable many people are about the business they run. I recently had a discussion with a man who has owned a men's clothing store for years. I asked him what it would take to start a business the size of his today? He began reeling off numbers for the cost of fixtures per square foot, the cost of initial inventory, and payroll expenses. He knew it cold. Discussion with several such business persons will be invaluable to you.

Operating Ratios

In addition to opening and operating expenses, you should quickly get familiar with retail operating ratios. Operating ratios are simply all the expenses accumulated in a particular account divided by the total sales for that same period of time. For example, in an apparel or clothing store, the cost of goods sold generally averages about 60 percent of business receipts. Whereas in a food store, it's more like 75 to 80 percent of business receipts. Operating expense ratios are available for many expense categories (rent, wages, bad debt, etc.) and for all types of retail stores. Two good sources are Robert Morris Associates' *Annual Statement Studies* and Prentice-Hall's *Almanac of Financial Ratios.* These may be available at your local library, or your banker and accountant (or future banker and accountant) might have copies of one or both. Knowing these ratios for your type of operation will help you determine if your business is on course. And if it is not, they will pinpoint the area to look into.

Specialized Operating Ratios

Most retailing business types have numerical "rules of thumb" which are used to determine a store's productivity. The most common of these ratios is sales per customer. It is easily obtained from daily records by dividing total sales for a day or week by the number of cash register totals for the same period. Knowing this value for your operation and for other similar stores can be very helpful. It can suggest that changes in store layout or merchandise mix (or some other variable that will encourage additional sales) are in order.

Sales-per-customer figures vary widely depending on the type of store. It is extremely low (about $1.50) for convenience stores, for example. A camera shop, furniture store, or clothing store would have a much higher ratio of course.

A second, specialized operating ratio in common use by retailers is sales per square foot of selling space. Again this value varies greatly, but to know it for your store and for similar stores can tell you a great deal. You can determine your store's value by dividing weekly sales by selling square footage. Noncompeting retailers will happily swap ratios with you.

If you're considering the purchase of an ongoing retail store, don't forget to calculate its sales-per-customer and sales-per-square-foot ratios. Then see how they stack up against your competition.

One last item on ratios. There is also a whole family of "balance sheet" ratios that are calculated for retailing businesses (as well as other businesses). Current assets to current debt, and current debt to tangible net worth are two common ones. My advice to you on these is to leave them for your accountant and your banker to worry about and advise you on. That is, unless accounting and finance are your specialty. These ratios and their implications are complex and best left to people who deal with them regularly.

Common Retailing Pitfalls

These are several areas where new retailers frequently make mistakes. Space does not allow for a detailed discussion of each of these areas, but I feel that they are important enough to highlight. In your research and learning activities, make sure you understand enough about each of these facets of retailing so that you can avoid costly difficulties.

Store design and layout   Have you ever gone into a store that was so confusing that you felt uneasy—a store whose layout burdened rather than helped you find the merchandise you wanted? You can avoid this problem by noting carefully the layout of stores you feel comfortable in and that you know are successful. Follow these principles when setting up or changing your store layout:

- Put impulse purchase items in highly visible and highly accessible areas (e.g., at the entrance).

- Design a layout that provides easy movement and minimizes congestion.

- Use display cases, racks, etc., that make it easy for customers to see the merchandise.

- Provide sufficient light and use lighting to emphasize particular displays.

- Make sure fixtures, colors, and furnishings are consistent with the image you want to project to the customer. Are you budget? Are you chic? Are you rustic? Are you quality at a fair price? Decide what *you* are and convey it in your design.

- Hire a highly recommended store layout expert, if you can afford one. Arrange a fixed price in advance. If you can't afford an expert, mimic, as well as you can, what you see in thriving stores.

Pricing Unprofitable pricing, whether too low or too high, can quickly drive a retailer out of business. Inadequate margins might provide high sales volume without sufficient profit. Unnecessarily high prices will lower sales volume below tolerable limits. Retail pricing is not extremely complicated, but it is complicated enough that it can be easily fouled up. Margins and markup, for example, sound as if they might mean the same thing, but they don't.

Then there's initial markup, shrinkage, loss-leaders, and markdowns. Carrying costs and turnover also have an impact on proper pricing strategy. If it seems as if I'm trying to make this seem at least a little complicated, you're right.

Mastering the art and science of retail pricing takes some practice and some effort. If I can coax you into doing your homework, you will be well served and I will feel that I've helped, in a small way.

Merchandise Selection Here is another retailing skill that you'll need to master. Of course, if you've had industry experience as a purchasing agent or merchandising specialist for a retail chain, or if you're planning to own a store that has a relatively short merchandising line, such as a pet store—you've got it made.

One approach to coping with merchandise decisions (as well as others requiring specialized knowledge) is to purchase a franchise in the retailing field. The franchise will provide assistance and guidance in this and many other operations.

However, if you don't do anything else, at least study the merchandise assortment of stores similar to yours. You can gain some benefit from their years of experience.

Ineffective advertising Some new retailers don't budget enough for advertising. Or if they do budget enough, as soon as things get a little tight, they cut back the advertising budget. Either of these actions is most likely a mistake.

Advertising is not a discretionary expense item. It's a *necessity* for most retailers. It's even more of a necessity for a new retailer or for a retail store under new ownership.

It's typical for an established small retailer (gross annual sales of $200,000 to $400,000) to spend between 2 percent and 4 percent of gross receipts for advertising and promotion. This translates into a minimum of $4,000 and a maximum of $16,000.

The type of advertising that you purchase is also critical to success. Four thousand dollars spent on ineffective advertising is four thousand dollars down the drain. Is price advertising best for your operation? Possibly promotion of a few lead items is best. Either find out or hire a competent, experienced advertising agency, at least in the beginning. Talk to some clients the agency has represented in the past, to confirm its competence.

At the startup of your business, plan to spend even more on advertising than the 2 to 4 percent. You'll need extra exposure to build awareness and store traffic.

A somewhat unique approach to advertising may also be appropriate for you to consider. In a Chicago suburb four independent food stores have banded together in an advertising cooperative. This has allowed them to purchase full-page ads in leading metropolitan newspapers. Their spending limits (of about 1 percent of sales) prevented them from doing this on their own. With an actual decrease in advertising expense, all four stores have experienced an increase in sales. Two of them reported weekly increases of over 20 percent.

This concept could work for any group of retailers who are distant enough so that their market areas did not overlap. In fact, I wouldn't be surprised to see imaginative advertising agencies offering some form of package deal to small retailers in the near future.

RESTAURANTS—YES AND NO.

Recently, an article in the business section of my local newspaper reported the opinions of several university professors. One was quoted as saying, "The independent smaller restaurant may just be on the way out."

The professor's reasoning for his conclusion went like this:

- Larger chain restaurants have the advantage of specialists who make operations effecient and economical.

- These specialists know exactly what equipment to install and how much food to buy, often at reduced prices.
- Fast-food franchises have the advantage of central purchasing and nationwide name recognition.

I agree, in part, with this analysis. But there is substantial evidence that refutes any suggestion of a quick demise of the independent restaurant.

Let's divide the restaurant business up into four segments and then I'll explain.

| | Future prospects | |
Service classification	Franchised and chain	Independent
Fast food	Good	Poor
All other (i.e., sit-down)	Good	Good

You can see from this little table that I project the prospects for *only* independent fast-food restaurants as poor. It is difficult, if not impossible, for an independent to compete successfully in this quadrant. The name recognition and the predictability offered by the franchises and the chains is overwhelmingly effective.

But, this is not at all the case for other types of independent restaurants. Sure, the other types of chain restaurants (e.g., Victoria Station, Beef & Barrel, Ponderosa) will do well in the future, but so will the independent restaurants that offer good food, efficient service, and competitive prices.

My prime evidence for this conclusion is in every city, every town, and every neighborhood of America. I can count literally dozens of highly successful independent restaurants within 5 miles of my home. There are two, no three, thriving combination coffee shop/full-menu restaurants right on the main street. There are three steak houses. Their parking lots overflow every night of the week. There are several ethnic restaurants that literally have no competition from chains or franchisers. I could go on and on. You can do the same thing in your town or in any town. In fact, many more successful sit-down restaurants are independent than are franchised or chain. According to a recent survey, food chains, including all fast-food restaurants, account for less than 35 percent of restaurant sales.

The reasons for the staying power of independent sit-down restaurants are many—including personalized service and individuality. When customers are spending $10 or more for a meal, most prefer a well-known, locally owned restaurant that has something distinctive and unique to offer.

Back to the quadrants of my table: The conclusion I'd like to get across is that a proven record of success exists and will continue to exist in three of four sectors:

- Franchised and chain fast-food
- Franchised and chain sit-down
- Independent sit-down

So if restaurants are your area, make a choice in one of these three quadrants.

Experience Needed—Sometimes

Prior restaurant management experience is critically important in certain types of restaurant ownership situations.

But, first let's look at the cases where it is not essential or maybe not even desirable. Bill Berger was a supervisor in a large manufacturing plant. He was fairly pleased with the job and his future was secure—or so he thought. A takeover of his company by a giant conglomerate changed all that. Reorganization began. Some jobs were phased out. Payroll was down by 30 percent at Bill's plant when he decided to act.

He found a job teaching vocational education in a high school (fortunately, Bill had gotten his teaching certificate before embarking on his corporate career). After less than 2 semesters of teaching, Bill knew why he hadn't become a teacher in the first place. He plain didn't like it.

It was at about this time that a friend asked if Bill would like to join him as a partner in a McDonald's franchise. Bill figured, "Why not?" They scraped up what savings they had, applied for a minority business loan and were on their way. Now, 5 years later, Bill is happy as part owner of three McDonald's restaurants.

If a highly specialized manufacturing supervisor/school teacher can succeed in the franchised restaurant business, it's safe to conclude that restaurant management experience is not essential there.

But this is not true in independent restaurants. Our college professor friends make this point strongly by saying, "People who go into the restaurant business without adequate training and experience are foolhardy. They will likely lose their shirt." This time I agree.

An independent restaurant operation is no place for a novice. An acquaintance of mine was a successful building contractor. During a recent building boom he was making money hand over fist by building custom single-family homes. For some inexplainable reason he decided to use his excess profits to build and run a white-tablecloth restaurant. He built a fine restaurant. But he didn't know how to run it. It lasted only 7 months. He sold it for well below fixed asset value. This man didn't lack desire or motivation. What he lacked was restaurant experience.

But if you have restaurant management experience (as well as the kind of motivation the contractor had), it can give you what's needed in the independent restaurant business.

Rich Webster is a perfect case in point. He's the classic example of the poor student who made it big. Rich openly admits that he flunked a lot of subjects in high school and flunked right out of college. Then at 24 he began working for his father as a restaurant manager. Six years later Webster felt he was ready to go off on his own. He and an old school friend decided to start a restaurant. They chose to go after the growing singles market. The location they selected was in the heart of a "with-it" neighborhood full of singles and young couples, many with sizeable disposable incomes and few with the time or the inclination to cook.

But since Webster wasn't used to dining out at lavish places, they decided to keep menu prices moderate. Webster's experience was apparent in everything from selecting equipment to picking menu items to hiring waitresses and waiters. The restaurant emphasized good food and good service and an enjoyable relaxed atmosphere. Two months after opening, traffic began to pour in. It hasn't let up since.

My wife and I had the place recommended to us. It sounded so good that we drove all the way into the city (more than 20 miles) just to try it. We waited 45 minutes for a table (no reservations accepted) and had a great meal.

Webster, 7 years after his first opening, now owns 8 successful restaurants with various partners. He coyly refers to sudden great prosperity as "a difficult phenomenon, which everyone should experience."

Personal Involvement

Seasoned restaurant people say they can't overemphasize the importance of personal involvement in the successful operation of a restaurant or other food service operation.

The most obvious reason for the owner of a new restaurant to be personally involved is to make decisions and keep things running smoothly. In restaurants, these activities require much more of a hands-on involvement than in other types of businesses. There are almost daily food and supplies orders, deliveries to be coordinated, new employees to be trained, equipment repairs to be supervised, and entries to be made in the daily register. Decisions must be made on everything from staffing to covering for a cook who hasn't shown up, to coping with an intoxicated customer.

Another important reason for a high degree of personal involvement is to keep employees functioning efficiently and to keep employee motivation at the highest level possible. Nothing accomplishes these aims as effectively as having the boss around. Restaurants are a labor-intensive business. If you don't believe this, just go into a McDonald's at lunch time and count the people *behind* the counter. Most restaurants spend between 30 percent and 40 percent of sales on food. But they also spend about 30 percent to 35 percent on employee wages and benefits. So from an expense perspective, food and employees are of about equal importance. From a practical perspective, how well the employees prepare and serve the food may have more impact on the success of the restaurant than the quality of the foods that are purchased.

A final contribution of personal involvement is the impact it can have on the customers. I personally prefer restaurants where I know the owner cares about me—not necessarily knowing me by name or even recognizing me because I've been there frequently, but conveying enthusiasm and concern through his or her presence. Some owners act as the maitre d'. Others stop at a table or two to say hello. Others have obvious "mother hen" rituals. In their own personal ways, they show that they care.

Partners

In many businesses, partners can be as much of a disadvantage as an asset. But partnership arrangements appear to have a lot going for them in the restaurant business. Many skills are required to run a restaurant successfully. Often one person possesses some of these skills but not all of them. Partners can frequently strengthen the ownership's overall capabilities.

Another strong reason for considering a partnership arrangement is the combination of long hours and personal involvement that are a part of this business. Many restaurants are open for 12 or more hours a day, 7 days a week, including holidays. A partner or two to share the load may greatly relieve this burden.

Finally, most restaurants take a good deal of capital to start. A 3,000-square-foot restaurant that seats about 90 will probably require $100,000 to $250,000 to start, depending on location, menu, etc. Two or three partners may be needed to raise needed capital.

MANUFACTURING—MAYBE.

One area of expertise that many people develop while working for a large employer centers around the production process. People become skilled machine tool operators, quality control supervisors, plant supervisors, machine maintenance and repair specialists.

Often these skills are transferable to one's own small business. And often people do start small manufacturing businesses that attempt to exploit manufacturing skills developed in industry. This is fine, if the new business is founded on the three elements that are essential for a new manufacturing business to succeed:

- A product
- A means of production
- A marketing system

John Korsky was a master machinist at a Ford transmission plant. He knew just about everything that anyone could know about production lathes. One day, John decided to venture off on his own. He leased a small building, purchased three used but high-quality production lathes, and opened for business. Ford had given him a contract to make a specialized, difficult-to-produce, transmission shaft. For John, this assignment was easy. He broke even in 2 months and was prospering in 6. Then the transmission that utilized John's shaft was suddenly dropped from the model line. John's contract was cancelled. He picked up several short-run jobs in the next months, but for the most part his machines were idle more than they were running. Eventually John Korsky closed his business and took a job as a machinist again.

Why did John's manufacturing business fail? I think it was because right from the beginning he lacked the essential ingredients for manufacturing success. In fact, from my point of view, I don't think that John was really in the manufacturing business. Actually, he was running a specialized job shop. He had no product and a poor (if any) marketing system. What he really was selling was a service—a manufacturing service. That's what job shops do.

Now don't misunderstand me. I'm not saying that a job shop is not a viable business opportunity. I'm saying that if one is in the job shop business, one must recognize this and act accordingly. Successful job shops sell service. And successful manufacturing companies sell products.

Manufacturing without Manufacturing

It's quite possible, maybe even desirable, to start and to succeed in the manufacturing business without doing any manufacturing.

Earlier, I listed three elements needed to succeed in the manufacturing business: a product, a means of production, and a marketing system. Too many would-be manufacturers concentrate on the means of production at the expense of the product and marketing, when, in actuality, the means of production is least important.

Nowhere is it written that a manufacturing company must actually manufacture its own products. And in fact, many of them don't. Take automobiles, for example. All the automakers purchase a large portion of their end products from other manufacturers. Pistons, brake components, even entire engines are purchased. Sometimes auto manufacturers purchase entire vehicles and just market them under their name. This is quite commonly done with foreign manufactured economy cars and light trucks.

You should seriously consider this same strategy. It offers several benefits:

- The efforts that should be devoted to marketing will not be diverted by putting out fires in manufacturing.
- Farming out manufacturing will lower your capital needs.
- It may also lower your breakeven point by lowering your overhead.
- It provides added flexibility.

There are companies that specialize in making products for other companies, who in turn sell the product to the eventual end user. Job shops are in this category. They'll make so many per month of whatever you need, whether it's a component for your product or the entire product. Finding a reliable contract supplier for your product should not be difficult.

Of course, you should realize that having someone else manufacture for you also has its shortcomings. You'll lose some degree of control over scheduling, quality, etc. And your unit cost could be somewhat higher since your cost per unit purchased will include your supplier's profit.

Fulfilling a Need

However you go about acquiring your product, don't fall into the trap of letting the product be an end in itself. The end or purpose of your business is *only* and I emphasize *only* to sell your "manufactured" product in sufficient quantities to make a good profit.

To meet this end, your product must satisfy a user's need. Here is a beautiful example. Over 20 percent of automobiles sold in the United States are manufactured overseas. Many foreign cars are underpowered with high-speed engines. For this and for a number of other reasons, foreign car engines frequently have a shorter life than the car itself. This raises a question. Which makes more sense: to buy a new car when the engine wears out or to buy a replacement engine at 10 percent of the new car price? No question. It's the engine. What we have here is a classic example of a *need*.

Four young entrepreneurs recognized this need and are fulfilling it. They are rebuilding Volkswagen, Datsun, and Toyota engines to the tune of over $2 million in sales per year. Each invested $10,000 in the business when it was started 5 years ago. This successful business also remanufactures foreign car engine components. These are sold to dealers and auto parts distributors.

The most unusual aspect of this company is that little effort has been put into sales or marketing. "All we ever had to do is satisfy the demand," says one partner. This can happen with the *right* product at the *right* time, but don't count on it. Instead, expect to have to push your product and push it hard. Even if it is a "better mousetrap."

The Export Market

Most young manufacturing companies have problems coping with their domestic market. Probably the last thing they want to do is get involved in exporting. But, the export market is one that should not be rejected without consideration. Several avenues are available to appraise the export market, including these:

- The U.S. Department of Commerce frequently brings foreign buyers together at trade shows in large metropolitan areas. Talking to foreign buyers could give you some idea of how your product might do in international markets.
- International trade clubs, made up of local business people involved in exporting, can be most helpful. The exposure and knowledge gained by attending a few meetings could assist you in judging foreign prospects.
- Short courses on foreign trade are offered in evening schools. These are often sponsored or cosponsored by international trade clubs, the SBA, or the Department of Commerce.

Many people in domestic small businesses feel that exporting is just too difficult. But there are experienced small exporters who know how to do it profitably. Give it a look. Then you can judge for yourself if it could fit into your business plans. You might read these two SBA releases:

- "Export Marketing for Small Firms"
- "Marketing Overseas with U.S. Government Help"

THE SERVICE BUSINESS OPTION.

The service sector of our economy is healthy and expanding. It provides and will continue to provide many excellent small business opportunities.

Service business possibilities are extremely diverse. Possibilities range from catering to dry cleaning, from car washes to landscaping to hundreds of other possibilities. Most of these will prosper in the future. A few will not. So evaluate your business choice wisely.

The beauty of many service businesses is that they require much less initial capital than other business types. This is true because many are labor intensive. The low initial investment requirements are

apparent when you look at what it takes to start a building maintenance service. It's possible to start and operate (for the first 3 months)
a commercial building maintenance company for about $10,000 to
$20,000. Still a lot of money, but much less than required in most
retailing and manufacturing businesses, for example.

The service sector of our economy seems to provide the opportunity for a continuous stream of concepts for new services. Here are just
three that I've heard of recently:

- A man opened a recording studio for amateurs and struggling professional artists. He rents the place and its equipment for $30 an
  hour and also produces finished tapes for his customers.
- A businessman started a restaurant referral service. For a $30
  yearly fee it allows members to select and reserve seats at any of a
  number of out-ot-town establishments that have been screened
  and selected.
- A couple started a consulting service that will assist well-to-do
  people in the selection, training, and communication problems associated with live-in help.

All are unique and appear to have at least fair probability of
success—because they satisfy an existing need. The ever-increasing
complexity and specialization of our economy will continue to provide opportunities for new service businesses. Keep in mind however, that the risk will be higher than if you enter a more traditional
service business field.

Traditional service businesses that offer a solid future include:

- Home remodeling and repair
- Residential or commercial cleaning
- Gardening and landscaping
- Electronics repair
- Day care/child care
- Temporary help (both secretarial and industrial)

- Catering food service
- Tax preparation
- Equipment/furnishings rental
- Interior decorating
- Car services (especially franchised outlets)
- Security services

This list is not meant to be exhaustive. There are dozens more. Browsing in the yellow pages of your local telephone directory will generate more possibilities.

The key to succeeding in a service business is to provide the benefits that you as a consumer would hope to receive from a company like yours. In other words, put yourself in the customer's position. For example, suppose your portable color TV goes crazy. What would you hope to receive from the repair shop you take it to? How about:

- A free estimate
- A firm estimate
- Prompt service
- Quality work
- Friendly atmosphere
- A decent warranty
- A fair price
- Honesty
- That little extra (free delivery, evening hours, candy for the kids, etc.)

How often have you found all these in your experience as a customer? Not often enough, I'll bet. That's why there is always a good opportunity in service businesses. If you provide your customers with these keys to service business success, 90 percent of the time you'll be on your way to success.

One more word: Service business owners who are making it are doing so because of the quality and enthusiasm of their employees. Almost all service businesses are labor intensive. Owners can't afford high turnover, shoddy work, etc. So they make it a point to develop their staff—to give them good training, reliable equipment, fair pay, and a sincere pat on the back once in a while.

The earning potential of the service business varies widely even within a specific type. For example, I know of two equipment rental franchises who represent the same franchiser. Both appear to have similar profit potential, yet one earned $14,000 last year and the other earned $65,000! The difference in bottom lines reflect the difference in the quality of service provided.

THAT GREAT IDEA.

The highest-risk approach to entering business is to start a new business from the ground up. And the highest-risk product is a new product. (Even major corporations have more new product failures than they have successes.) So, what do you get when you put the two together? That is, when you start from the ground up a new business based on a new product? That's right. Very high risk! There are just no two ways about it. The chance of failure with this combination is much higher than the chance of success.

But people will always have ideas for new products and new services and the potential rewards that our free enterprise system offers will always be tempting. So in this section I'm going to outline a systematic approach to help control the risks of new-business–new-product ventures.

Preliminary Idea Evaluation

It is difficult, at best, to evaluate without bias one's own new idea. But there are several things you can do that will help.

The first is to let time take its toll. Brand-new ideas, like brand-new romances, are impossible to judge fairly. Write your idea down as descriptively as possible when it first appears. Then think about it for at least a month. Whenever new aspects or ramifications come to you, write them down. After some time passes, look over all your notes and ask yourself:

- Does a real need exist for the idea?
- If not, is it desirable? (No one needed a Pet Rock, but thousands bought one.)
- Roughly, what do I think it would take to manufacture it?
- What price would consumers be willing to pay for it?

Now if you're still enthusiastic about your idea, *do not* submit it to any company that places invention-wanted ads in magazines and newspapers. If you do, you just might end up spending $500 or $1,000 or $2,000 to hear and read about how great your idea is. These companies make their living by building up the ego of would-be inventors. And they charge a handsome fee for it. If you want your ego expanded, just tell your wife or a friend about your idea. They'll tell you how fantastic it is—for free!

This raises another point concerning unbiased evaluations. You probably won't get any from family or friends. So don't even try.

One place you may be able to turn to is the Innovation Center at the University of Oregon. This center, established with a $1-million grant from the National Science Foundation, judges the commercial feasibility of over 500 new inventions a year. Whether the foundation will still be around when you read this book, I can't say, but it's worth a letter or a phone call to find out.

Preliminary Plan

If, after your soul searching, you still are optimistic about your idea, it's time for some detail work. At this stage you've got to turn your idea or concept into something tangible:

- Drawings or sketches
- Detailed description (for a service)
- Mock-up or prototype

Having accomplished that, you can turn to cost estimates. If you're without background or experience in this area you'll have problems, but do your best. One way to estimate costs is to compare yours with existing products. If your product is no more complicated than some item selling for $9.95, then you can safely assume that your product could be produced and sold profitably at $9.95.

Business cost estimates should include all the following categories:

Materials   Determine material prices by calling suppliers. Check low-quantity and high-quantity prices. Get quotations if you feel you need them.

Production   Labor and equipment will be necessary. Determine competitive labor rates and price the equipment items needed.

Packaging   Most items require packaging. Retail items probably will require attractive, professionally designed and produced packaging. Don't forget packaging labor costs.

Marketing cost   This will be the most difficult to estimate. But a good safe figure is 15 to 25 percent of your eventual selling price.

Overhead   This includes rent, owner's salary, utilities, and all the costs not directly included in calculating the production costs.

Some estimates of sales volume are needed to determine each of these costs on a unit-cost basis. I'd use an estimate that translates into at least a $50,000 per year sales volume, maybe even $100,000. You shouldn't even be contemplating a business unless it promises to generate $50,000 to $100,000 in sales. And as sales go up, unit costs go down. So, a conservative sales estimate ($50,000 to $100,000) will prevent you from estimating unrealistically low unit manufacturing costs.

Cost estimates and your "best guess" estimate for a realistic selling price will tell you where you stand on profitability.

The final phase of the preliminary plan focuses on marketing. Can the product be sold best through the mail, direct to retailers, or through manufacturers' representatives? Who specifically is the target customer group? Homemakers living in apartments? Teenagers? Golfers? Who are they and how do you best reach them?

It's all beginning to sound awfully complicated, isn't it? Believe me, it is. And I'm only touching on each critical topic. Big companies have experts or even groups of experts in each of these areas. They have cost estimators and design experts and full-time market researchers. See the Appendix for a description of how big companies develop and market-test new packaged-goods products. It will give you additional valuable insights.

I hope you're beginning to doubt the wisdom of starting a new company based on a new product. Whether you are or not, stay with me a little while longer. It gets more hopeful, I promise.

Patents, Copyrights, and Trademarks

It's time to get all the protection you can for your idea. And don't try to do it yourself. If you believe in your idea, you must spend the money to protect it: See a reputable patent lawyer. Lawyers are listed in the yellow pages. Call several, ask for related experience and references, then select one. Take in your preliminary plan and seek guidance. A patent on a relatively simple concept will cost you $400 to $600, maybe $1,000 on the high side.

Selling Your Idea

We're now up to the more hopeful part. And I'm going to illustrate it with a personal example. For me, writing is a business. It helps support me and my family. Each manuscript is a unique new product that is untried in the market place.

Basically I have two choices in marketing a manuscript. The first choice is to do it myself. I can hire a compositor to set it in type, design a jacket, and have it printed and bound. This would cost me about $10,000. Then I could market the book myself, either by direct mail, through book distributors, or maybe even direct to big book chains. This marketing effort, complete with advertising, would cost me at least $5,000 to $10,000. Writers have produced their own books, and a few have even succeeded in marketing them in quantity. In fact, several of the highly successful "happy talk" small-business books that I've been knocking are new-product—new-business ventures. If I could sell 100,000 books and net $2 per book, I'd be on easy street.

But my risks would be high. I'd be investing $15,000 to $20,000. I'd be bucking the major publishers who put out over 30,000 new hardbound book titles each year. These firms are fighting for shelf space in stores and for customers. What chance would I have against the giants of the publishing business? They have market muscle, dozens of salespersons, experts in direct-mail campaigning.

So what is my other choice in marketing a manuscript? That's right. Sell the rights to the book to a publisher in exchange for a royalty. That's what I do. I risk no capital and I gain the marketing strength of my publisher.

You can do the same thing with your new product or service that I do with manuscripts. It will relieve you of a lot of headaches, and it will save you from the rip-off artists I describe in Chapter 7. The basic steps include:

* Choosing your target companies
* Developing a presentation
* Making contact
* Negotiating

You'll be expected by companies to sign an idea submission form. If your product is accepted, a fair royalty is about 5 percent of factory gross sales.

There are several good books on the subject of new products and how to market them to companies. I recommend *How to Turn Your Idea into a Million Dollars* by Don Kracke.[1] It has one of those titles I abhor, but inside it has a good deal of sound advice.

Going It Alone

It's not easy to sell a new-product idea to a big company. Just as it is not easy to sell a manuscript to a publisher. If you fail to sell your

[1] Don Kracke, *How to Turn Your Idea into a Million Dollars*, Doubleday, 1977.

new-product idea or choose not to sell it, you've either got to give up or you've got to go it alone.

Just because companies have rejected your idea doesn't mean it's no good. Here's a case in point.

Phil Tillins is a retired shopkeeper. One day he noted how much trouble his young grandchildren were having with the blocks they used to build bridges and buildings. The blocks kept falling apart. But the children were too young for sophisticated building sets.

Several years and countless hours of tinkering passed before Phil had his new building set designed and debugged. "It was unbelievably difficult to get into toy companies," Phil said. "But I did eventually get to present my idea to three major producers." All three said they liked it, but all eventually rejected it without explanation.

So Tillins decided to go into business for himself. He contracted with a small plastics firm to make parts and used a handicapped organization to package them. Tillins then talked an independent toy distributor into taking on his line in the Chicago market.

You know what? It's selling very well. In the product's first 6 months about 10,000 units were sold for $14.95 each. This healthy beginning gave Phil the clout he needed to get a major TV promotion company to take on his product. It is now on the shelves at Sears, Ward's, and Penney's.

It probably won't be long before toy companies are making offers to Phil Tillins. He admits he'll probably sell out. "Let them run with it," he says. "I'm too busy inventing. I've got another new toy I think they'll be interested in, too!"

FIVE

Buying a franchise.

Probably the most anxiety-free and possibly the most risk-free way to get involved in a business is to purchase a franchise.

CONSIDER THE ALTERNATIVES.

Before we get involved in the ins and outs of identifying and buying a sound franchising opportunity, I want to make a point about the entry options that are available when you go into business for yourself. The point is that you can enter most types of businesses by one of three routes:

- Acquiring a franchise
- Buying an ongoing business
- Starting from scratch

Obviously, this is not the case for *all* businesses. But it is for the most popular. Look at Table 1 on the following page. It shows the six major business types discussed in the previous chapter. Notice that there are at least two and often three ways to get involved in any of these business areas.

Table 1 Alternate Entry Routes

	Franchises	Ongoing	Startup
Mail order		X	X
Retailing	X	X	X
Restaurant	X	X	X
Manufacturing		X	X
Service businesses	X	X	X
New idea		X	X

The message here should not be overlooked. Too many fledging entrepreneurs naïvely believe that the only way to go into business is to start a business from scratch. This route could lead to disaster, because actually the most risky and complicated way to enter business is to start from scratch. Similarly, the most complicated and worrisome way to become a home owner is to have a home custom-built. Without question, it is safer and easier to purchase a condominium (not unlike purchasing a franchise) or an existing home (not unlike purchasing an ongoing business).

Another mistake some people make when entering a business is to assume—wrongly—that the route they choose is a decision "forever." Not true. You could start by buying a franchise, selling it (hopefully at a profit) two years later, and then starting another business from scratch. In the same way, you could buy a condominium, sell it two years later, and then have your dream home custom-built.

I'm not going to devote space here to the pros and cons of the three ways of entering a business. Much of that is included in other small business books. But if you are truly unsure about the best route to take, I'd suggest you read my *How to Pick the Right Small Business Opportunity.*[1] The early chapters of the book describe a straightforward way to sort out all the relevant considerations.

---

[1]Kenneth J. Albert, *How to Pick the Right Small Business Opportunity,* McGraw-Hill, 1977.

BE LEERY OF SMALL BUSINESS TRADE SHOWS.

The business opportunity show or exposition is described in many small business books as a good place to search for franchising opportunities. I'm afraid that I can't agree with this advice. The shows I've been aware of over the years have not lived up to expectations. Their major deficiencies include:

- High-pressure sales techniques by many exhibitors
- Too many vending machine routes or rack jobbing positions (These can be valid business opportunities, but they are not appropriate for many people.)
- Some exhibitors pushing "starter product kits" for $3,000 to $4,000 or more (These kits are so profitable that the exhibitors have little concern for your ultimate success; your initial purchase has already put them on easy street.)
- Inconsistent quality of the seminar presentations
- Few high-quality franchising opportunities on exhibit

Small business shows can be a good learning experience. You are exposed to all kinds of people and all kinds of opportunities in a few short hours. But if you do attend, be prepared to say no when offered that "once in a lifetime opportunity."

GOOD PLACES TO FIND OPPORTUNITIES.

With less effort than it takes to attend a small business exposition, you can uncover more franchising opportunities than you'll know what to do with.

Franchising directories   Several directories are published that list and describe hundreds of franchising companies. You can find these at your local business library.

The Wall Street Journal   The Thursday edition usually has several pages of ads placed by franchisers. Remember, the companies advertising there are aggressively soliciting new franchisees. Some of the large, well-established franchising companies don't need to place ads because their reputation by itself can attract large numbers of potential franchisees.

Local newspapers   Most large metropolitan newspapers have a fair share of franchising opportunity classified ads, usually in the business opportunities section. Most likely, franchising ads in local newspapers are placed by companies that are small and not well established.

The telephone directory   The yellow pages of your local telephone directory is a great place to look for franchising opportunities. Turn the pages and note the ones that appeal to you. The great advantage of the yellow pages is that you'll see the franchisers that aren't out hustling for new franchisees. McDonald's, Wendy's, Servicemaster, and other large, successful companies need new franchisees just as much as the ones that advertise in newspapers. Calling up or writing the ones you're interested in is worth the effort. You may be just the person they are interested in.

DON'T GET OVERWHELMED.

There are hundreds of franchise opportunities, in all types of businesses, in all price ranges. Because of the almost infinite choices available, some people get overwhelmed by it all. You can avoid this by narrowing down the field to three or four franchises in two or three different types of businesses. You can use some form of screening criteria or you can do it quite arbitrarily. It's OK just to say, "These are the only types of franchises that I'd be interested in operating, so they are the only ones I'm going to investigate."

It's also a good idea to set up a schedule for contacting and evaluating franchise opportunities. Make it realistic and specific. Budget 1 week for contacting companies, 2 weeks for preliminary contact, and maybe 6 to 8 weeks for investigating the ones you like.

NEW OR ESTABLISHED FRANCHISES?

When selecting your initial list of franchising companies to contact and investigate, you'll need to consider the track record of each franchiser. Then the question becomes do you select new, unproven franchisers or do you concentrate on well-known, highly successful ones?

The obvious answer is to go with the well-known, highly successful companies. But this might not be the right answer for you. Successful, well-established companies typically charge more for their franchises and offer less profit and growth potential than new franchisers do.

A McDonald's franchise is a sure thing, but it's expensive and most of the choice locations are gone. Another way to go is to seek out the McDonald's-type success story while it's still unknown and unproven. Sure the risks are higher, but the entry cost is much lower and the potential rewards are greater.

The investment requirements and earnings potential of selected franchise can be seen in Table 2.

THEM EVALUATING YOU.

You can contact most franchising companies either by mailing in a coupon requesting information or by calling a toll-free telephone number. This step will produce a phone call to you or a packet of information in the mail, followed by a phone call. Either way you'll quickly get the feeling from the phone call that you are a job applicant rather than a potential franchise purchaser.

In the initial contact you may be asked some rather personal questions, such as whether you have the needed $18,000 (or whatever) to invest, or whether you have experience in this or that. This job-applicant feeling will intensify at your face-to-face meeting. You'll fill out applications. You'll quite likely be asked to take a barrage of tests. By the way, some franchising companies insist that you take

Table 2 Investment Requirements, Annual Sales, and Net Return of Selected Franchise Opportunities

Franchiser/Description	Investment		Average annual sales range	Net return on sales, %
	Cash	Total		
KOA/campgrounds	$ 60,000–$75,000	$250,000–$1 million	$ 75,000–$1 million	25–50
McDonald's/fast food	$125,000–$140,000	$250,000–$275,000	$700,000–$900,000	7–11
General Business Services/ small business services	$ 20,000	$ 20,000	$120,000–$150,000	50–70
Midas International/ car repair	$ 50,000–$ 60,000	$100,000–$120,000	$200,000–$500,000	9–11
White Hen Pantry/ convenience store	$ 8,000	$ 20,000–$ 25,000	$450,000–$500,00	5–7

their tests; if you refuse, you're immediately dropped from consideration.

The best way to cope with the franchising company's evaluation process is just to go along with it. It's understandable that franchisers must screen their potential franchisees. After all, their success ultimately depends on the success of each franchisee. In fact I'd be leery of a franchising company that didn't do a thorough evaluation; such companies are either careless or only interested in pocketing your franchise fee.

If you dislike the feeling of being an applicant, that reaction might tell you something about your ability to enjoy and adapt to running a franchise. Every franchisee pays a price in more than money for the priviledge of operating a franchised outlet. The price involves giving up some freedom and autonomy. If the franchiser's selection process seems too much like a job application process, then owning and running a franchise might strike you as too much like being an employee. For you, having a totally independent business might be the right way to go.

YOU EVALUATING THEM.

Although it's critical for you to be accepted by franchisers, it's even more critical that you do a thorough and meaningful job of evaluating them. Fortunately, the parallels between applying for a job and buying a franchise don't hold at this point. It's difficult to get incisive, straight-forward information about a particular job opening, but this is not the case for information about franchise opportunities. With good planning and a little digging, you can gather the facts and opinions necessary to make an intelligent choice.

Begin by developing a list of questions to ask each franchiser. You'll want to take these with you to your personal meetings. Here are some basic questions that should be on your list:

- How long has the company been in business? When did it award its first franchise? How many franchises are there now? Are they distributed regionally or nationally?

- At what rate have franchises been added in the past? How many new ones are planned for this year? Next year?

- What policy changes—specifically related to new products, advertising, programs, and franchise services—are being considered for the near future?

- How does the franchiser view its competition? Which company is largest? Most aggressive? Is any new competition on the horizon? What are competitors' strengths and weaknesses?

- In a privately held company, who are the major shareholders? Were they the original founders?

- How much and what kind of assistance is available to new franchises for establishing facilities? Are facilities usually purchased or leased? Is a feasibility study of the location provided? How about construction guidance and assistance?

- What territorial rights are granted to a franchisee? Is the franchise exclusive or nonexclusive? In a two-step distribution system, are you being offered a distributorship or a dealership?

- If any portion of the initial franchise cost is to be financed, what is the interest rate? Is any of the initial cost refundable in case of cancellation?

- How many franchises have failed? Is the failure rate changing? How does the franchiser explain these failures?

- Ask for names and addresses of operating franchises in markets similar to those you are considering. Also ask for names and addresses of franchisees who have failed. (There should be no hesitance in supplying these.)

- Has a franchise ever been assigned for the market you're considering? If so, what was its fate? If it is in operation, ask if you could visit the owner.

- What is the training program like? How long does it last? Where is it held? Who pays for it? What topics are covered? Are there any training aids available for training your own employees?

- Is there an ongoing training program for franchisees? If so, is it a scheduled or impromptu format? What topics are covered?

- For nonstore franchisees, how is the selling accomplished: door to door, company-supplied leads, or prospecting? Do competitors use the same approaches?

- Ask for an explanation of the franchiser's advertising program. Is there advertising and promotion support available for local advertising by the franchisee? Is a local advertising agency required or suggested?

- What services and ongoing assistance are offered by the franchising company? What about central purchasing, problem analysis, field service personnel, order expediting, and so on?

After meeting with several franchisers, you should be able to distill the potential franchise opportunities down to two or three top possibilities. Then, evaluate them by gathering further information from three categories of franchisees for each company:

- Current franchisees
- Failed franchisees
- Franchisees of competitors

Develop a list of questions for each category of franchise operators. For example, here are questions for current franchisees of a company:

- When did you buy this franchise? What was your background and prior experience?

- What were you looking for in this franchise?

- What is your territory? Is it exclusive?

- What is your personal work schedule? Does it vary much from day to day? When are the busiest periods?

- Exactly what products and services does your franchiser supply? Is the delivery timely?

- Whom do you consider your strongest competitor? Why? What do they do better than your franchiser?

- How would you characterize your relationship with your franchiser? Has it changed of late? Is their product-quality good?

- How often do they visit you? Do you consider most visits helpful or intrusions on your business?

- Do you have any specific problems with the franchiser?

- Do you have any major problems with the business itself?

- What is your opinion of the company's national advertising program? What about local advertising assistance?

- How good is the company's training program? Is the training updated to keep pace with changes in the operation?

- Is the company's site-selection system good? How would you characterize the demographics of your site? Are you happy with this location? Why?

- What do you think of your fellow franchisees? Are they happy with their situations?

- Are you familiar with any franchisee failures in this chain? Why do you think they failed?

- Are you happy that you bought this franchise? Would you do it again today? Why? Why not?

- Can a franchise in this type of market area reach the sales-goal estimates made by the franchiser?

- How about the profit figures?

- Could you give me a rough estimate of the annual sales of your franchise? What does it net before taxes?

- Is your sales volume growing? How much of this is price increases? Are your profits growing?

You'll need to get answers to all these questions. The only way is to call up franchisees on the phone, tell them that you're thinking of buying a franchise, and ask if you can visit them sometime soon. Ninety percent of them will be happy to help you. In no time you'll know almost as much about each franchiser on your list as they know about themselves.

THE UNEASY ALLIANCE.

Recently, the *Wall Street Journal* ran a front-page article about the friction that sometimes exists between franchisers and franchisees. In the first paragraph, the article notes that "sometimes the two are barely on speaking terms."

The most likely area of dispute is the threat of termination of licenses or nonrenewal when the current license expires. Some franchisees contend that franchisers trump up petty reasons for discharging a franchisee because they (the franchisers) want either to resell the franchise at a higher price or to turn it into a company-owned outlet.

There is a trend in the fast-food segment of franchising to more company-owned outlets. Franchisers now own about ¼ of all outlets as compared with ⅛ 10 years ago. Company-owned outlets are typically more profitable to the franchiser, so the reason for the trend is apparent. Some franchising companies are now so large that they have the financial muscle to open their own outlets rather than sell franchises.

You should investigate this aspect of the franchise opportunities you're looking into. Ask the franchisers about their practices and future plans. Ask the existing franchisees for their opinion. But keep in mind that there will always be some unhappy franchise owners. Some people just like to gripe, especially about "headquarters." So talk to enough people to get a balanced response.

Also examine the franchising agreement of several franchisers. Compare sections dealing with grounds for termination and transfer of ownership.

PICKING A WINNER.

Here is a simple checklist to help you pick a winning franchise opportunity. If you have solid answers to each question and if you compare the answers of several franchisers, you should make an intelligent choice.

Checklist for picking a franchise:

1.   Does the franchise appear to satisfy most of the elements I am looking for in a business?

2.   Do I have the necessary capabilities to succeed in a franchise of this type?

3.   Specifically, does the size and profitability of a typical franchise fulfill my income requirements?

4.   Does the franchising company have a reputation for honesty and fair dealings?

5.   Is the franchising company successful and profitable?

6.   Is the franchiser well established and experienced? If not, do they offer an unusually attractive opportunity?

7.   Does it appear to have the management depth to continue operations indefinitely?

8.   Have I been offered an exclusive franchise? If not, what guarantees would I have concerning sales potential?

9.   Under what circumstances could I terminate the franchise contract? What costs would be involved? When could they terminate me?

10.   To whom and under what terms and conditions could I sell my franchise?

11.   Is there a realistic and enduring need for this business in my area?

12.   What are my chances for meeting local competition?

13.   Is there a good chance of success in the territory offered me?

14. Has the franchiser investigated me thoroughly enough to satisfy itself that I can profitably operate one of its franchises?

15. Is there a good record of success among new franchisees?

16. Does the franchiser have a good training program for me? For my employees?

17. Is the advertising, promotion, and merchandising program satisfactory?

One last bit of useful advice on selecting a franchise: It may be a good idea to "dry-run" in your mind the actual activities involved in operating a specific franchise. In addition to doing the things you normally do in your regular routine, imagine the things you would be doing if you were operating such-and-such a franchise. Do this every hour or so for 2 weeks. This will give you a good way to determine the business's appeal. If, after 2 weeks, the business is still appealing, you'll know more surely that it's for you.

SIX

Buying an ongoing business.

Six years ago Bob and Betty Coulter did something extraordinary. They bought a business that was failing. It wasn't even a glamorous business like a boutique or a record shop. It was an appliance repair shop, of all things.

The Coulters were convinced that they could turn the business around. They knew there was a great demand for economical, reliable repairs of small appliances. And they knew that the manufacturers of these products (mixers, hair dryers, blenders, etc.) weren't doing a good service job. They were convinced that the business they bought had been loosing money because of inept marketing, not because of lack of demand. The business cost them all of $3,500, including repair equipment and a sizable parts inventory.

Several months after the purchase, the business was at breakeven. Soon after that it was thriving—supporting a family of four quite comfortably. They repair almost all types of small electrical appliances—coffeepots, lamps, air-conditioners, toasters. Everything except radios, TVs, and stereos.

DIAMONDS IN THE ROUGH.

Why do I say that the Coulter's purchase was extraordinary? Simply because many potential small business owners are almost petrified at the thought of purchasing an ongoing business—especially one that is failing!

But the purchase of an ongoing business is actually safer than starting from scratch. And the potential gains from acquiring a failing business at a bargain-basement price and turning it around can be more than worth the risk.

I'm making this point because I feel it's a message that hasn't been presented before. Most books on small business concentrate on starting a business from scratch, or emphasize the advantages of purchasing a franchise. I say, starting from scratch or buying a franchise is fine, but taking over an ongoing business, whether prosperous or a diamond in the rough, is also fine.

WHY AN ONGOING BUSINESS?

Besides the possibility of purchasing a turnaround situation, why is it a good idea to consider acquiring an ongoing business? There are several reasons. Let's look at them, one at a time.

Avoiding startup headaches   Starting a business from scratch is difficult and time-consuming, especially if you are working full-time or have never done it before. You've got to locate a site, investigate it, and negotiate for a lease. You need to purchase fixtures and equipment. You have to set up an effective, timely, record-keeping system. An advertising and marketing program must be planned and initiated. I could go on and on. Many of these activities are one-shot affairs. You do them to get started, then put them aside and do other things to run the business effectively. So much of the startup effort is somewhat akin to overhead; it's always there but it doesn't contribute directly to producing sales and profits.

Avoiding startup cost   All kinds of one-time costs are associated with starting most business, and they can really add up. I know of a pool and patio construction company that is now for sale in California. Its books show a total startup cost of $29,000. Many of these are one-time expenses that the sellers have no way of recovering in their selling price of $32,000. The selling price has been based on the current and expected earnings of the business. So the buyer of this pool and patio construction company will be saving many startup costs.

Avoiding fatal startup mistakes   An ongoing business with an established track record has obviously not committed any fatal startup mistakes—mistakes like poor location selection, improper merchandise selection, unprofitable pricing, or inept advertising. But many people who start a business from scratch do commit fatal mistakes. Sometimes it only takes one misjudgment at a critical stage to do in a new business.

Gaining instant customers   The customer, to paraphrase an old saying, is king. They are what every successful business has in quantity. Established businesses have customers! In most ongoing businesses, a change of ownership will not disturb the existing customer base. So the new owner of an existing business acquires customers along with the business. And along with the customers comes sales revenue and income. This doesn't necessarily happen when one starts a business from scratch.

Buying a known commodity   In one sense, buying an ongoing business is not unlike buying a franchise. Granted, it's a unique franchise with a single outlet, but like a franchise, you can tell what to expect. An ongoing business can be observed and analyzed before purchase. Its books, inventory, facilities, even its customers can be examined.

PITFALLS WITH ONGOING BUSINESSES.

Later in this chapter is a section explaining how to investigate ongoing business opportunities. At this point I want to emphasize that purchasing an ongoing business may not be without its hazards. That's because when you buy an ongoing business, you must take the bad along with the good. And some of the bad, like irreversible mistakes made by the previous owner, may not be correctable. The most obvious "bad" in any kind of retail or restaurant operation is location. Moving a business is difficult and costly. So don't purchase a potential turnaround business if you suspect that the location or some other irreversible situation is responsible for the poor performance.

Another hazard to watch out for is the contribution made by the present owner. Typically, when you buy a business the seller walks out the door and with him or her goes years of experience, expertise, customer contacts, etc. Some businesses (personal service businesses such as consulting) are very difficult to sell for this reason. Sometimes a workable solution is to offer the seller a multiyear employment contract. This provides time for a smooth transaction. Another possibility is to arrange for the seller to stay on for several months. Of course, you have to compensate the seller, but this arrangement is quite common.

HOW TO FIND GOOD OPPORTUNITIES.

Many books on small business recommend the most likely places to uncover ongoing businesses for sale. These include:

- *The Wall Street Journal*
- Local newspapers
- Realtors
- Business brokers
- Trade associations and publications

But you can find some real winners among ongoing business opportunities in two other little-known ways.

The first is word of mouth. Many business owners do not want it openly known that their business is for sale. They may be just close-mouthed or possibly don't want their employees to find out. Whatever the reason, the only course left to these sellers is word-of-mouth advertising. They tell their banker, lawyer, stockbroker, insurance man, accountant, and close friends at the country club that "they might be interested in selling." So what you should do is go around to these same people and tell them that "you're thinking of buying." With a little luck you'll find out about a purchase opportunity that not many other potential buyers know about.

The other technique is to take the offensive. Say, for example, that you want to buy a small retail store in the suburbs of a large city. You take out the yellow pages and look up the names and phone numbers of stores in the category you are interested in. Then you simply call up each store and ask for the owner's name and where you can reach him or her. When you get the owner on the telephone just say "I'm interested in buying a _____ type of store and I wonder if you know of any that might be available." I'll give you 10-to-1 odds that after a dozen or so phone calls you will have discovered at least one good lead. I've used this technique successfully to discover business purchase opportunities for clients and even to find a home for myself and family!

The beauty of this approach is that there is little or no time pressure involved. Since the owner is not formally offering the business for sale, you can usually have all the time you need to make a careful and thorough analysis.

ANALYZING ONGOING BUSINESS OPPORTUNITIES.

Once you've found an ongoing business that looks attractive, it's time to begin the analysis. I suggest doing it in two steps. The first step is the preliminary analysis. Its purpose is to give you enough information to decide whether your first impression (i.e., this is an attractive opportunity) was correct. The second step is an in-depth investigation of all facets of the business.

Step 1. Preliminary analysis   Begin by examining all the available records of the business in question. In some smaller businesses, financial records may be incomplete or ineffective, but glean what you can from them. Make it a point at this time to examine thoroughly income tax returns for the preceeding 5 years. These are usually good indications of a business's track record, especially since it is quite common to state gross income conservatively and to minimize net income by including any and all deductible expenses.

While you are examining the records, look over the facilities and operations. Check the inventory, the equipment, anything inside the company that will give you insight into how it is being run. It is best to do this alone. Ask the owner whether you might just browse around for a few hours or even a few days.

The final item you'll want to examine in your preliminary analysis is the external environment of the business. Talk with the company's lawyer, banker, and insurance agent. Make a point to talk to several major suppliers and to some customers. There is no need to disclose your actual purpose with suppliers and customers. Say that you're a consultant or with an advertising agency or taking a survey or whatever suits the circumstances.

After completing the preliminary analysis, you should be able to conclude one of three things: This is a thriving business. This business has problems, but maybe, just maybe, I can turn it around. This business is a loser; forget it. Obviously, if your conclusion is either the first or second of these three, you'll want to proceed to the indepth investigation.

Step 2. In-depth investigation: Several aspects are included in this investigation.

The first is to hire a competent certified public accountant (CPA), someone knowledgeable about the particular type of business. If you don't know such a person, seek one out. Ask the CPA about prior experience and references.

Your CPA should know what to examine and investigate, but make sure he or she covers:

- Pricing (You don't want any unfilled orders at prices lower than the market price, for example)
- Accounts receivable (age, probable bad debt, etc.)

- Inventories (obsolescence, valuation, etc.)
- Tax returns and tax liabilities
- Payroll, workmen's compensation (and other accounts)
- Income statements and income forecast
- Balance sheet ratios

You'll also want to hire a lawyer: first, to check everything from leases to zoning to patents, etc.; second, to help you in neogtiations if you decide to proceed with the purchase.

Another step in your investigation is to examine all the personnel records. Analyze the government labor regulations that affect the business. Check union controls, if any. Look at the wage rates and payroll. Make a point to engage some of the employees in an open and candid discussion.

A complete examination of the facilities and equipment may be in order. If you don't feel qualified to to this yourself, an equipment company representative or somebody else with the required expertise should be invited to help.

The last major area to investigate thoroughly is the company's competitive environment. This involves indepth discussions with the company's suppliers and customers. Customers will be especially helpful in industrial and service businesses. Also at this time make it a point to talk to people who are operating businesses similar to the one you are thinking of buying. Tell them some of the things you've learned about the business in question (you can keep its identity secret) and ask for reactions, comments, comparisons, opinions. This is a good way to get a solid indication of the company's reputation, strengths, weaknesses, future prospects, etc.

With all this in-depth investigation work, you should also be able to discover the real reason or reasons, why the business is for sale. The owner may have been telling you the truth, or he may not. In either case, a thorough investigation will tell you what you need to know to make a wise decision.

MANAGING THE TURNAROUND BUSINESS.

The initial, overwhelming advantage that you bring to a business that is not living up to its potential is objectivity. As soon as you begin your preliminary analysis, you will recognize opportunities for improving the business. As obvious as these opportunities seem to you, it's important to understand that they are probably either unnoticed or intentionally ignored by the present owner. No one likes to admit shortcomings or failure. But this is exactly what the present owner would have to do before taking positive steps to improve the business.

Signs of a Turnaround Situation

Before we get into the best approach for managing a turnaround situation, let's look at signals that you indeed have found a turnaround business.

1.   Decreasing sales: If sales are declining after adjusting for inflation, something is wrong. Also compare the company's sales with similar businesses, or use comparison ratios, such as sales-per-employee or sales-per-square-foot for a retailing business.

2.   Loss of market share: This is more difficult to measure, but if it is available or estimable, it is a telltale sign that competition is expanding more rapidly than the business in question.

3.   Falling profitability: Take note if absolute profit, profit per dollar of sales, or return on investment are declining.

4.   Changes in financial policy: If, for example, the business increases its reliance on debt or decreases the share of profits it reinvests in the business, something may be going sour.

5.   Management shortcomings: Lack of planning, a "know-it-all" attitude, indecisiveness, unwillingness to recognize problems—all are symptoms of a business that may be turned around by a change in management.

I want to emphasize that just because a business exhibits one or more of these signs, it doesn't necessarily mean that you or anybody else will be able to turn it around. These signals just mean that there are problems. Finding solutions and implementing them successfully is what makes a successful turnaround. Let's look at how this can be done.

Accomplishing a Turnaround

Identifying problems is the first essential step, as I stated above. The next step is to gather relevant facts and opinions that can contribute to finding a solution. This should be accomplished as part of the in-depth investigation. Also, at this time (i.e., before you make a commitment to buy a business) you should analyze all the information available, compare alternative solutions, and decide on an appropriate turnaround plan. This plan should detail specifically what you expect to do after you purchase the business. It should detail the expected results and the time when each is to be accomplished.

A major decision is in order at this point. If, after you've completed your analysis, you haven't been able to pinpoint problems and develop a high confidence level solution, what do you do? The business is tempting, with great potential in your estimation, but you are not quite sure how to turn it around. If you get into this position, my advise is to decide *not* to purchase the company. It just might be that the present owner is already making the best of a bad situation. Possibly circumstances beyond his or her control (and possibly beyond your control)—such as, competition from foreign suppliers—are blocking meaningful improvement in profits.

If, on the other hand, you feel confident that you can turn the company around, then go ahead and do it. I know of a man who bought, at a real bargain price, a small specialty paper products company that was not doing well. He was sure that more aggressive sales techniques could significantly expand sales and profit. He bought the company, and you know, he was right. In 3 years, sales doubled and profits quadrupled (because overhead increased very little). Now he has a happier problem to cope with: expanding plant and equipment capacity to keep up with sales!

Usually a successful turnaround is accomplished by determination and focus. You must be determined to see it through to a successful conclusion, and it's critical that you focus the turnaround effort on just one or two problem areas. These should be areas that offer the quickest and greatest potential for improvement. Discontinuing all products or services that are not carrying their weight may be the answer. Or an effective advertising program might do it. Whatever you do, don't spread your effort around. To reiterate: concentrate on the one or two problems that will make the biggest difference in the success of the business.

One last item! You may be entering a situation filled with tension and anxiety. Any carry-over employees will be worried about their future. This is true in any change of ownership, but it is especially true for a business that's less than healthy. The best approach is to be candid and honest. Tell your new employees as much as possible concerning your plans for the company and for them. This will prevent exaggerated rumors from spreading via the company grapevine.

VALUING AN ONGOING BUSINESS.

The fair market price on an ongoing small business is one of the most nebulous of all business valuations. A case can be made for pricing many small businesses either as low as liquidation value or as high as 20 times future earnings, even if present earnings are negative.

I know one broker of small businesses who hesitates to show a prospective buyer the books for the businesses he handles until after the prospect has seen the business and talked to its owner. This broker's philosophy is that in many instances the books, especially the income statement, will not be able to justify the asking price and, therefore, will turn off a potential buyer. What this broker is *really* saying is that often he sells the "sizzle" rather than the substance of a business. Watch out for this. There is often only a fine line between a business with true potential and a lemon with sizzle.

Asking prices for small businesses are just that—asking prices. The best way to determine the true value of a business is to gain experience by shopping around. You'll begin to learn how to detect those businesses with inflated asking prices. In reality, the only true valuation is the price someone is willing to pay. Good bargains are had when the buyer relies on good business sense rather than emotions.

There are established formulas to determine a fair selling price in some types of businesses. It would be well to inquire of business brokers and business owners whether such a method exists in the type of business you're investigating. Also, some books may be available at your local library that specifically deal with established methods of valuing particular types of businesses and properties. One of these is *Guide to Buying or Selling a Business*[1] by James M. Hanson.

Beyond specific formulas and established tradition, there are two basic approaches for estimating a fair purchase price. The first method is generally referred to as capitalization of future earnings. You may be familiar with this approach from reading the financial press, because it is the method used in acquisitions by most big businesses. A modification of it is also used in the stock market. In this context, expressions such as "it's selling for five times current earnings" or "seventeen times estimated earnings" are common.

Capitalization of Future Earnings Approach

This approach is based on two estimates. The first is an estimate of a business's future annual earnings, usually for 5 years into the future. The second estimate is a quantification of the risk associated with the business. This risk factor is usually estimated by comparing the business with the known risks of other types of investments. If the business is stable and secure, for example, the risk might be similar to a bank savings account or U. S. Government bonds. Suppose this return is 5 percent. Then, if the business has a 5-year estimated future

[1] James M. Hanson, *Guide to Buying or Selling a Business*, Prentice-Hall, Englewood Cliffs, N.J. 1975.

pretax profit of $5,000 a year (after deducting the owner's salary), this approach leads to a fair market price of $100,000, which is $5,000 divided by 0.05 (the return rate). However, if the risk is much higher, the risk factor might be estimated at 25 percent. Then the business would be valued at $5,000 ÷ 0.25, or $20,000. Big businesses usually think in terms of return on investment rather than risk factor, but it's really the same process. In the last example, if this business were purchased for $20,000 and earned $5000 per year, the annual return on investment would be $5,000 ÷ $20,000, or 25 percent. Either way, using risk factor or return on investment, the results are the same.

Asset Appraisal Method

The second method of estimating a fair market price of an ongoing business is based on asset appraisal. The tangible assets most commonly involved in the transfer of a small business are inventory, office supplies, fixtures and equipment, and possibly real estate. The one intangible asset is goodwill. Valuation of all of the tangible assets is fairly straightforward, although an expert appraiser often is called in to assist on inventory, equipment, or real estate. After all these tangible assets are appraised, an additional value is added for goodwill—such items as favorable location, customer lists, special connections with suppliers, capable staff and personnel, reputation, and so on. All these goodwill assets relate to the future earning power of the business. Typically, the value put on goodwill is less than half, frequently only 10 or 20 percent, of the total value of physical assets.

Drawbacks of Both Methods

It may be obvious by now that both these methods have shortcomings. The capitalization of future earnings method requires that both future earnings and a risk factor be estimated. This makes its application, in many situations, nothing more than a guessing game. The use of historical data to forecast earnings is often impossible because of the absence of either good records or earnings or both. Moreover, a relatively small change in the risk factor can significantly affect the resulting fair market price. A change, in risk factor from 7 percent to 14 percent, for example, cuts the price in half.

Because of the nebulous nature of this first method, the asset appraisal method is used more frequently. Of course, its major shortcoming is the difficulty of assigning a mutually accepted value to goodwill. Potential buyers rightly value goodwill with respect to future earning potential. But sellers often want to associate the value of goodwill to past investments of time, effort, and money.

Excess Earning Method

Happily, there is an approach that resolves some of the shortcomings of dealing with either method, because it's actually a combination of the two. It seems to be the most reasonable approach, and I would advise its use in most instances. This combination approach, often called the excess earning method, starts by sharply differentiating a business's salary income from its investment income. It assumes that buyers quite naturally look for a business that can earn a fair return on investment, after deducting a reasonable salary for themselves and for any time put in by their family. This after-salary income (or income potential) must be at least equal to the earning power of outside investments, or the buyer would have no interest in making a purchase.

Let's look at an example of the excess earning method. Assume that the tangible assets of a business are fairly valued at $100,000. Assume also that the buyer is looking for a 10 percent return on investment, roughly comparable to the return expected from a high-quality common stock. Ten percent of the $100,000 asset value is a $10,000 annual return, or profit on investment. The potential buyer feels that the full-time effort in running the business is worthy of a salary of $20,000 a year. Therefore, the buyer expects a pretax total net profit of $30,000 each year ($10,000 + $20,000). The next step is to compare this $30,000 figure with the actual (or anticipated) profit of the business. Suppose this well-established business earns $32,000 a year, on the average. Subtracting gives an excess profit of $2,000 ($32,000 − $30,000). By projecting this excess profit over some time period, the value of goodwill can be determined. The time-period multiplier depends on how long it would take to establish a similar business and bring it to a similar level of profitability. Assume the buyer places the value at three years. Then goodwill, in this example, has a value of $6,000 (3 x $2,000). So the fair market value of the business is $106,000 ($100,000 physical assets + $6,000 goodwill).

Let's also look at the implications of a lower average earnings figure. Assume, for example, that the business averaged a profit of only $25,000 instead of $32,000. Then the excess earnings would be negative ($25,000 minus $10,000 return on investment and minus $20,000 salary = − $5,000). This negative excess earning implies at least one of these conclusions:

1.   The assets have been valued too high.

2.   The assets cannot earn a 10 percent return.

3.   The business cannot support a $20,000 owner's salary.

4.   The full earning potential of the business is not being realized by the present owner.

In any case, the business, as currently constituted, is worth something less than the appraised asset value of $100,000. If the profit picture cannot be improved, the business will not meet the prospective buyer's requirements for return on investment and salary. This example points out one of the advantages of this method. It requires a potential buyer to examine profitability, return on investment, and salary—independently.

In some purchase situations, it may be useful to consider one other figure: the liquidation value of assets. It represents the amount that the assets of the business would bring if it were liquidated. This is usually the rock-bottom price for which a business can be purchased. Many businesses that are in a loss situation or whose owner is eager to sell can be bought for something around the liquidation value. Knowing this figure for a particular business may help in price negotiations.

GAINING THE MOST ATTRACTIVE TAX ADVANTAGE.

It's possible to allocate the purchase price of an ongoing business to give you, the buyer, attractive tax advantages. Your CPA can assist you in this area, but here is a sampling of the concepts involved.

If your purchase price includes a covenant with the seller not to compete with you, spell out the price separately from the price of goodwill. Be specific about the sum and the period of the contract. Then you may be able to deduct this payment over the term of the agreement. Attempt to value long-life buildings, improvements, and equipment at a low level. Then you will have a long depreciation over which to recover these costs, while possible losses on the sale of the long-life assets will still be fully deductible. On the contrary, short-life assets—machinery and equipment—should be valued at a high price. Short-period depreciation permits cost recovery quickly.

The process of value adjustment and negotiation goes on and on. New that you're aware of it, you can handle it at the appropriate time.

USING OWNER FINANCING.

Frequently, because of the federal capital-gains tax laws, the sellers of businesses are interested, even eagerly, in providing financing for your purchase of their business. They get a tax break if your down payment is 29% or less of the purchase price. Often owner financing is offered at lower interest rates than bank financing. And, of course, the interest costs are tax deductible. So always query the seller early concerning the possibility of owner financing. This could make the purchase of an ongoing business even more attractive.

SEVEN

Starting a new business.

You may have gathered by now that I'm generally not in favor of a newcomer starting a business from scratch. But in some circumstances this is the only way—or the best way.

WHEN TO START FROM SCRATCH.

There are no reliable data on the number of first-time business owners who started their business rather than purchasing a franchise or an ongoing business. But the available data strongly suggest that most first-time business owners start from scratch. In fact many people never even consider any other route when they think about going into business. To me, this is illogical.

Because of the higher risk and more complicated nature of starting from scratch, it is my feeling that one should embark on the startup course only after careful consideration. Here are the factors that I think are important:

1. As I've emphasized, franchising is the lowest-risk way to enter business; every potential businessperson should explore the possibility of buying a franchise. Talk to a few franchisers in areas that interest you. You'll know quickly if this is a viable route for you.

2. Consider buying an ongoing business. If you want to run a bicycle sales and repair shop, for example, it may be better to buy one, if you can. I've already cited all the advantages of this course in the last chapter.

3. Examine your personal needs. Is it important to you to have total independence? Do you treat your business as an extension of your thoughts and ideas? Do you always push to do things "your way"? If you answer these questions yes, then starting from scratch may be the best route for you.

4. Is your business concept built around a new product or new service, one that doesn't now exist in the market, like the Frisbee or the Pet Rock? Or, is it a new concept in catering or a clever and useful new household gadget? If this is your situation, then you obviously have no choice but to start from scratch.

5. Another sound reason for starting a new business is insufficient capital. Many new businesses can be started for a lot less money than it takes to purchase most franchises or ongoing businesses. Recall the used-car appraisal business I described in the first chapter of this book. It was started by two men who each put up only $750.

6. A final factor to weigh in your decision to start from scratch is the size of the business. Many small new businesses, like the one I just mentioned, can be started with a modest commitment. If you can start small with your business concept, you won't be risking very much, so you wouldn't have that much to lose if you fail. This point is covered in more detail in Chapter 8, Entry Strategies.

KEEP IT LEAN AND FLEXIBLE.

What is your image of the work environment and creature comforts of a successful independent management consultant? A person who advises top companies? A big, well-appointed office in a new high-rise building? A private secretary, even an assistant or two? This may be how some consultants spend their hard-earned money, but I know one shrewd fellow who has quite the opposite philosophy. Bill Morgan is his name, and lean and flexible describe him exactly.

Since almost all his meetings and contacts take place at his clients' facilities, he sees no need for a fancy office. In fact, his office is a 10 by 15 area in the basement of his home. It's pleasant, well lighted, with its own phone (and phone number), and the rent per month is *zero* dollars.

Bill has no secretary. Instead he hires a typist by the hour to do correspondence and reports. An answering service handles his phone calles when he's away from his "office."

"I wanted to keep the overhead down when I started the business," Bill explains. "A downtown office, furniture, a typewriter, and a secretary would have cost me well over $1,000 a month. I couldn't afford it then, and now, I guess, I'm too cheap to spend it. I've got other things that I'd rather spend $12,000 a year on—like a European vacation or my sailboat. And you know what? The clients of mine who know I operate out of my basement respect me for it. They know I'm not wasting *their* money. If we need to meet here in town, I rent a motel conference room for the day, or I reserve a room at the airport. That's more convenient for them anyway."

Bill Morgan's philosophy is one that I think everyone starting a business from scratch should adopt. It goes like this:

- Keep your overhead (fixed-cost items like rent and equipment) to a minimum. This will lower your breakeven point.
- Avoid unnecessary frills. Fancy stationery, for example, does nothing more for your business than simple stationery, except to give you an ego trip.
- Don't hire anybody you can't utilize fully. Don't hire over-qualified people. They cost more. Use part-timers or even temporary help. This keeps you flexible.
- Consider a full-commission compensation system for your sales people, if you have any. Then you'll only have to pay for what

they produce. Marketing through manufacturers' representatives is an extension of this approach.

- Consider renting or leasing your equipment. This will conserve capital and allow you to discontinue costs associated with any equipment you no longer need.

RESIST TEMPTATION.

Too many people who start businesses from scratch cannot resist the temptations associated with the first signs of success. Starting a business is a trip into the unknown. It creates anxiety. The first days or months of operation may be filled with tension and apprehension. New owners ask themselves: "Will people really come into my boutique and spend money?" Or, "Will I have the right parts to fix those bicycles?" Or, "Will department stores order my new widget?" When a new business owner is sure the answers to these questions is an emphatic yes, he or she breathes a big sigh of relief: "You know, I really am going to make it."

This is when you need to resist temptation. Don't expand too rapidly. Don't buy that Mercedes you've had your eye on. Don't hire two extra people.

Instead, go out to dinner with your spouse. Celebrate. Order steak or lobster and your favorite bottle of wine. You deserve it. Maybe even go to the theatre. You deserve that, too. Blow $100 or even $200. So what! Then go home and go to bed. You'll sleep well knowing you're making it, rather than worrying about what will happen if your expansion doesn't fly, or whether you bit off too much with that Mercedes or those two new employees.

DON'T REINVENT THE WHEEL—USE IT.

Are you thinking of starting a new business that's similar to other existing businesses? If so, that's probably good. It will probably lower your risk and improve your chances of success. Let me explain.

Existing businesses that resemble your new business can tell you two things:

1.   Of foremost importance: you can learn whether a consistent *record of success* exists for these businesses.

2.   If you're satisfied, about the success record, *duplicate in your business* the key conditions that have contributed to others' success.

Let's examine these points in more detail.

A Record of Success

Personally, I would never start a new business that is similar to other existing businesses unless I were sure the other businesses have been consistently successful. Just because a group of businesses exist, it doesn't necessarily follow that they are successful, will be successful, or will even continue to exist.

The existing businesses may be just eking out a subsistance wage for the owners. Or, a change in the competitive environment may be taking place that will severely dampen profitability in the near future.

If you're starting your "similar-to" business after personal experience working in that industry, then your acquired knowledge will tell you whether a record of success exists and is expected to exist in the future. But if you're starting your similar-to business without such personal work experience, you'd better seek to understand the record of success and the basic reasons for it *before* you launch your own enterprise.

You can do this by aggressively seeking out the facts.

- Gather industry estimates and statistics.
- Talk frankly with trade associations.
- Question owners of existing businesses.

Note: As long as your business is far enough away or different enough from theirs that you don't pose a threat, most owners (I'd estimate 9 out of 10) will gladly share their insights with you.

Duplicate Success in Your Business

An old expression says it all: "Imitation is the sincerest form of flattery." Go ahead and imitate the factors that contribute to the success of other business. For example, if a good location is a key factor in the success of similar businesses, then seek out a location with similar characteristics (automobile traffic count, demographics, median neighborhood income, etc.).

Don't let vanity or pride stop you from copying. That's just plain foolish. As long as you do no harm to people already in the business, don't worry about it. It's done all the time. Fast-food franchisers are a perfect example. When one franchiser found that an eating area in the store and drive-up windows increased sales, they all started adding these features to new outlets.

The franchise concept itself is the epitome of duplication,—or imitation or copying or whatever you want to call it. Ray Kroc saw how successful the only McDonald Brothers' hamburger stand was, bought rights to the concept, and has literally duplicated it thousands of times all over the world. I'd like to get in on some of that kind of copying myself! Wouldn't you?

HIGHER RISK—HIGHER REWARDS?

At the other extreme from the "similar" situation is the "original concept" situation.

Here's a perfect example. Until about a year ago Hank Ross was a young, married, handsome construction worker—also, an avid runner. Hank had an idea. He called it the Jogger's Water Belt. The need for it is straightforward: running makes one thirsty, but runners don't want to stop to take a drink. Even if they did, there is often no appropriate liquid refreshment around. That's where the water belt comes in. It's a lightweight, clear plastic tube that straps easily around the waist. Attached to the main tube is a thin plastic tube that runners can put in their mouth and suck on whenever desired. A good idea? A viable product? A good business opportunity? To tell the truth, I just don't know. I don't think anyone can know for sure, yet.

Hank thinks he has a great idea. He feels that it will appeal not only to joggers, but also to bicyclists, hikers, golfers, tennis players, motorcyclists, and even construction workers who can't leave their work place for extended periods.

Hank has turned his idea into a reality. Nine months of experimenting and testing at a workbench in his living room has resulted in a cost-effective, functional design. As a matter of fact, with present tooling he can produce 700 to 800 belts a day right in his livingroom!

I'm sorry but I can't tell you if this story has a happy ending. It's too early. The Jogger's Water Belt is just going on the market. Hank's father, who has experience in retailing, is handling the marketing and promotion. *Runner's World Magazine* is doing a feature article on the testing of the belt in its next issue. That publicity will surely help.

The belt is being offered in several colors and comes complete with a plastic funnel and hose to aid filling. The belt and its accessories are packaged in a plastic resealable pouch. Suggested retail price has been set at $12.95.

Hank now has all the ingredients for a successful company, except the most elusive one of all—customers. Will enough people shell out $12.95 plus tax to make the Jogger's Water Belt a winner?

Let's assume a set of cost and margin values and see what they tell us. Here are the *assumed* values per unit:

- Production cost: $1.25
- Marketing and overhead expense: $2
- Selling price to retailer: $6.50
- Profit: $3.25 = $6.50 - ($1.25 + $2)

These values are somewhat typical for specialty consumer products. If Hank's company sells 10,000 belts a year, it will gross $65,000 ($6.50 x 10,000) and net a profit of $32,500 ($3.25 x 10,000). Not bad. But remember this profit is all-inclusive. It must be divided up to cover return on invested capital, owner's salary, and bottom line business profit (the risk profit over and above a fair return on invested capital). Now the $32,500 looks somewhat more modest. As a matter of fact, it's probably the bare minimum that would be needed to legitimately call the business a success.

Now let's look at the potential upside reward. Let's just suppose the belt is a booming success. More and more people are jogging—kids, executives, homemakers, senior citizens. Literally millions of people are taking up jogging, and all of them get thirsty.

So what if yearly sales of Jogger's Water Belts are 100,000 instead of 10,000? Then sales would be $650,000 and profits $320,000. Fantastic!

Is this realistic? I doubt it, but who knows? Hank is taking a higher risk by starting a business around a unique and unproved product. These kinds of ventures usually also have higher *potential* rewards.

BEWARE OF RIP-OFF ARTISTS.

Rip-off artist is the descriptive label given to the unscrupulous business person who illegally duplicates someone else's successful product. Let's assume, for example, that Hank's Jogger's Belt begins to sell well in the five western states where he will begin distribution. The word quickly gets around that it's a winner. Lucky Hank. He's got it made. A successful product with a brand-new patent—the protection of the U.S. government for his creation.

Would anyone dare steal Hank's idea? You bet. In a short time a rip-off artist could come out with a product similar to Hank's and have in it *national* distribution, skimming the cream off the entire U.S. market. Of course, Hank could sue, but legal action takes months, often years. There are motions and countermotions, delays, appeals.

This exact thing happened to a man in Portland, Oregon. After 3 years of legal battles, he settled out of court for $75,000, of which his lawyer got ⅓. During that time the rip-off artist sold $6 million of the product in question and made hundreds of thousands of dollars in profit.

In an earlier section of this book, I recommended modeling your business after a successful one that already exists. As Richard Nixon would say, I want to make one thing perfectly clear: I do not condone or recommend that you extrapolate this advice into becoming a rip-off artist. There is a world of difference between duplicating a thriving model of success (without harming other existing businesses) and an outright theft of someone else's idea.

Guarding against Rip-Offs

There is no sure way to guard against rip-off artists, but there is a strategy that you should consider. Instead of marketing your product idea on your own, patent it, then sell the manufacturing and marketing rights to a large, reputable, nationwide company. This type of arrangement can give you marketing muscle that you couldn't possibly develop yourself. Your large partner could saturate the market before competitors could react. Besides, rip-off artists are somewhat more hesitant to take on "big guys" with high-powered legal departments.

Although this approach may lower your potential upside profits somewhat, it provides another side benefit. It eliminates most of your headaches. You won't have to worry about raw material supplies or prices, employee absenteeism, or equipment that breaks down at the worst times. All you'll have to do is cash your royalty checks!

ESTIMATING YOUR MARKET POTENTIAL.

Estimating the success of an untried new product is difficult at best. Again let's take the Jogger's Water Belt as a case in point. There are three primary ways to test the market potential of this product, all simple and relatively low cost.

Retail Test Market

Sporting goods stores and department stores will probably be pleased to cooperate in a test. I'd give each retailer a dozen belts on the condition that they offer them at the suggested retail price. First,

I'd see how they do with no advertising support. I'd try this for 2 or 3 weeks. Next, I'd place an ad in the sports section of a local newspaper, listing the stores where the product is available.

This technique applies to almost any retail product that can be produced and packaged for testing in small quantities.

Direct Marketing

The mail-order appeal of the Jogger's Water Belt can be tested by placing an ad in a metropolitan newspaper or a runners' magazine. Another possibility is to purchase a list of 1,000 names and addresses of known purchasers of, say, running shoes. This list will cost about $30. Sometimes the returns from a simple brochure or a descriptive letter will give a good indication of direct market potential.

Direct Retailing

I'd try to sell the water belt at a major running event that attracts a large audience. These are held more and more frequently. Just set up a sales area, put up a sign, and see what happens. It might also be worth trying this approach at a main street or shopping mall sidewalk sale. The one disadvantage of this method is that it probably is least representative of a viable, large-scale marketing channel. On the other hand, it does provide an opportunity for on-the-spot feedback from consumers.

To quantify your estimates in each market channel, fill in a forecast table like this one:

	Forecasted Sales in Each Year (Units)				
Market channel	1	2	3	4	5
Retail					
Mail order					
Direct					

INDUSTRIAL PRODUCT MARKET POTENTIAL.

It's also possible to test the market potential of new untried industrial products or services. In this method, however, a transaction is not consummated. Rather, an appointment is made to visit a buyer or purchasing agent just to talk about your new concept. During the visit, you describe the product or service. The company representative has a chance to comment on the desirable features of the concept and express an intention of interest.

This technique is used by all major industrial product companies. It works for them and it will work for you.

EIGHT

Entry strategies.

Let's presume that you've decided to go into business. You know the kind of business you would like to own and operate. You've checked it out and are confident that it is a type of business that will prosper in the future, and that you'll enjoy it.

So you're ready to start. What do you do? Well, what else! You do whatever it takes. You sign the franchise paper and go off to training school, while your franchiser searches for a site. Or you seek out a business to buy. If you are starting from scratch, you locate and lease a site, purchase equipment and supplies, hire people. These actions are soon followed by a gleeful announcement to friends and fellow employees: "Guess what, I'm going into business for myself." Your resignation letter precipitates rounds of congratulations, handshakes, and farewell parties. Then, at last, one Monday morning you're unlocking that door, putting your new "Welcome, we're open" sign on the window—and you've done it. You're in business!

This is the way we all see it happening. And many people enter businesses just this way. But it is far from the only way, and for many of us, far from the best way. In fact, so far from the best way that this approach is frequently the main contributor to failure.

Actually, there are many approaches or strategies for entering small business. In this chapter the basic ones are presented and highlighted. Consider each carefully and then decide which one or combination of several is right for your situation and your business.

THE UMBRELLA STRATEGY.

Have you considered franchises and decided they are not for you? You want total independence, total freedom to run *your* business the way *you* want. Yet, on the other hand, you are apprehensive about going it alone. Your wife or husband is afraid you might lose tens of thousands of dollars in your dream business. After all, you don't have any direct experience in sports equipment retailing or operating a country inn, or in whatever business you'd like to enter. If this is your situation, then consider this strategy. First, you buy a modestly priced yet successful franchise in your chosen field, or directly related to it. This allows you to learn from experts. You'll get training, guidance, and helpful advice in all facets of managing a small business. You'll be making money and learning at the same time. Then in several years you'll have these choices:

- Stay with the franchise and possibly expand it or purchase another. You've found out that franchising isn't really that constricting. You like it.
- Keep the franchise but hire a manager to run it for you. It's become a good money-maker and a good investment.
- Sell the franchise and apply your experience and capital to that dream business you wanted in the first place.

Many new business people make the mistake of assuming that the first business choice they make is *forever*. That simply is not true, especially in today's dynamic business market. You can and maybe should make the transition from employee to employer one step at a time. Franchising offers the opportunity to do that.

THE START-SOMETHING STRATEGY.

Suppose your plans for going into business are stymied by one or more of the following roadblocks:

- Inadequate capital
- Serious family problems (e.g., pending divorce)
- Only a few more years on your present job to qualify for a pension
- Total inexperience in business
- A spouse who puts job security or job status before your need for fulfillment and achievement
- A handicap or illness
- Fear of failure
- Inability to decide what type of business you'd like to be in
- A procrastination complex

My advice to you is to follow the "start-something strategy." The "something" business to start can be any number of kinds, but it should be something that:

- You can operate from home
- Requires a low capital investment
- You can manage in your spare time
- Fits the space available in your home

Don't be concerned about the nature of the business itself. It doesn't necessarily have to be related to the kind of business you eventually want to own. That would be nice, but it is not necessary.

Don't be too concerned about the income potential of your something business. Since most at-home, part-time businesses are labor intensive, your income will be limited. Just accept this.

The purpose of this type of start is not to make lots of money or even to lead directly to a business that does. Rather, its purpose is to get you started—now. It's something to give you confidence, if you need confidence. Or to give you some experience, if you feel that's what you need. It's a start—nothing more, nothing less.

There are literally hundreds of something businesses to choose from. Some that come to mind are:

- Roto-tilling service
- Garage sales
- Typing service
- Day-care service
- Fishing tackle repair
- Firewood sales
- Antique restoring
- Crafts

As soon as you think of a business that will get you going, go ahead and start it. You'll be risking very little besides your time and effort, and it could be "the start of something big," as the song lyric puts it.

THE BUILD-UP SLOWLY STRATEGY.

Another business entry strategy—related to but distinct from the start-something strategy is the build-up-slowly strategy. In this approach you are starting the business that you hope will become a big winner, but you start on a small, low-risk scale. Elements of this strategy include:

- Starting part-time
- Keeping your present job
- Keeping overhead to a bare minimum

Say, for example, that eventually you'd like to own and operate a bicycle shop. The *classic* way to approach this business would be either to purchase an ongoing shop, quit your job, and—presto—go into business; or to lease a store front, purchase fixtures and merchandise, hire clerks, quit your job, and—presto—go into business. But either approach could be dangerous. You'd be risking tens of thousands of dollars and giving up job security.

Instead, why not *build up slowly?* Start with a bicycle repair shop in your basement or garage. Join some bicycle riding clubs. Maybe you could pick up a line or two of bicycle accessories to sell to bicycle shops and enthusiasts as another step in the building process.

There is a couple in Texas who implemented the build-up-slowly strategy. She worked in an office at the time, and he was a college student. The business they chose was mail-order fruitcakes. The first year they sold only about 200 cakes for a gross of $800, with a profit of about $300. But each Christmas season they expanded. Soon they were up to 900 cakes in a selling season. Seven years after starting their business, they finally moved out of their home into a 7,000-square-foot baking and shipping facility. Twenty years after startup, the business is now selling 160,000 pounds of cake a year. Gross sales are just over $400,000. That's what can be done with the build-up-slowly strategy.

One point I want to emphasize is that this strategy can and should be used in conjunction with the other entry strategies discussed in this chapter. Whenever possible, it is *always* best to start small, keep your present job, and build up slowly.

THE FIRST-LEARN-SELLING STRATEGY.

The essence of success in small business is selling. This message is developed completely in the last chapter of this book.

The first-learn-selling strategy suggests that since selling is so important, you should learn it before becoming self-employed, and then build a full-blown business around your selling skill.

There are several ways to go about developing sales skills, and all of them depend on firsthand experience. Sales expertise cannot be learned in a classroom. If it could, the dropout ratio among newly graduated real estate and insurance salespeople wouldn't be so high.

The first and most direct way to gain sales experience is to get a full-time sales job. Of course, this option has its drawbacks. It requires that you give up your present job, and that your age, past experience, and education fit available full-time sales openings. But if you know the type of business you want to enter and can gain direct sales experience in this or a related business, by all means do it.

A second way of implementing the first-learn-selling strategy is to keep your present job and take on a second, part-time sales job. The idea is to match as closely as possible the sales expertise you need and the type of sales experience available in various part-time positions. For example, if you're interested in owning a retailing business, an evening or weekend sales job in a similar type store would be perfect. Other part-time sales positions which may be applicable to your needs include:

- Direct cosmetics sales (e.g., Avon)
- Real estate sales
- Rack jobber route

The rack jobber option needs some explanation. Rack jobbing is a specialized marketing technique. Rack jobbers set up display racks in retail outlets, stock them with merchandise, and then periodically check and restock the racks. Sales generated from the rack merchandise are shared with the retail store owners, according to various formulas. Commission rack jobbing routes are available for products ranging from candy to panty hose. Companies that have routes available can be found at local small business opportunity fairs. Retailers will also be able to supply the names of rack jobbing companies. The most challenging sales aspect of many rack jobbing sales routes is persuading a retailer on the benefits of having your rack in his or her store.

THE GET-TO-KNOW-YOUR-BUSINESS-FIRST STRATEGY.

This strategy is an extension of the first-learn-selling strategy. It suggests that if you're going to enter a particular type of business, it might be a good idea to get to know that business first. The obvious way to implement this strategy is to get a full-time or part-time job in the chosen business, just as you would do to gain sales experience.

This need not take years of effort, however. It might even be possible to gain the needed experience in several weeks. A woman in New Jersey did just that. She wanted to start a domestic service, one that could provide reliable, high-caliber house cleaning. To get to know the business, the first thing she did was to get a job cleaning house. It wasn't hard. In fact, the service that hired her didn't even interview her thoroughly. After a week of work assignments varying from a half-day to a day-and-a-half, in three households, she felt she knew what it was like to be a house cleaner.

Next, our domestic service owner-to-be tried the other side of the business. She contacted three domestic services told them she was a homemaker, and requested a domestic worker to come in once a week. She asked about the services they offered, prices, etc. The lack of professionalism on the part of these businesses astonished her. She knew then that a top-notch domestic service would succeed. She hired one house cleaner from each service so that she could get direct insights into her potential competitors techniques and personnel.

She now felt ready to start her business. From voters' registration list, she got names and addresses for a mailing to affluent neighborhoods in town. This mailing offered top-quality domestic workers and a money-back guarantee. The telephone hasn't stopped ringing since. Her domestic service now employs over 350 workers and grosses over $300,000.

THE SPOUSE-SUPPORT STRATEGY.

The spouse-support strategy is a takeoff on the old story of the wife who puts her husband through school by working while he studies. Except that in today's society, spouse support works either way: the wife works to support her husband's business venture, or the husband's job supports his wife's business entry.

The primary advantage of this approach is obvious. It provides a regular paycheck that can at least pay for bare necessities such as food and housing. This steady income takes much of the pressure off of the partner who is involved in a new business. It allows him or her to make long-term decisions in terms of what's best for the business, rather than what's needed for supporting a household.

The spouse-support strategy will only work with the full cooperation and understanding of both partners. It goes almost without saying that it shouldn't even be attempted if the relationship is the least bit shaky. The financial pressures and time demands of a new business could be enough to destroy any relationship that doesn't have a solid foundation.

THE SAVE-AND-STUDY STRATEGY.

As you may recall from an earlier chapter, inadequate initial capital is a major cause of failure for new businesses. So if you don't have the necessary capital and you can't raise it anywhere, you should postpone your business entry and set up a monthly saving program instead.

During the time it takes to accumulate adequate capital, you can do other constructive things. For example, you can:

- Take an evening course in bookkeeping, marketing, etc.
- Read at least 1 book every 2 weeks that will contribute to your business knowledge base
- Study your future competition by
  —analyzing newspaper advertising
  —visiting stores three times a week to observe merchandise movement, instore promotions, etc.
  —subscribing to trade magazines and journals
  —talking to and learning from suppliers, accountants, bankers, lawyers, and customers

All this learning will make you a better businessperson when you have accumulated the necessary money. And it will accomplish something else, too. It will help keep alive your hopes and dreams and savings program. Without the learning activities, you could easily lose sight of how much you really want your own business. This could lead you to skip making regular deposits in your future business account. Worse yet, it could lead you to chuck your dream and spend the money you've accumulated on a vacation or other frivolous things.

THE TEAM STRATEGY.

The topic of partners is a popular one in many small business books. The advantages and disadvantages of having one or more partners have been hashed and rehashed. But you should consider some special aspects of partnership arrangements as part of your startup strategy. These aspects are:

1.   Having two or three partners could allow you to start a full-time business without giving up your present full-time job. Your partners can also maintain their job security. For example, three partners started a men's clothing store. They hired a clerk-manager to handle the store from 10 A.M. to 5 P.M. on weekdays, and they took turns covering the store on evenings and weekends. They also divided the advertising, stock control, bookkeeping, and office work.

2.   Consider the possibility of having a silent partner. Many affluent people are willing to invest in sound business ventures. They're not always easy to find, but the benefit of substantial financial backing may be well worth the search effort.

3.   It is often possible to get your feet wet in a business situation by becoming a minority or junior partner. You won't have much say-so in such a situation, but you could get a lot of high-level exposure and experience in a short time.

NINE

Financing: problems and opportunities.

Many small business books, unfortunately, are extremely idealistic when dealing with the topic of new small business financing. These books spend dozens of pages describing in detail how to organize and write a formal business plan. This plan, as the scenario develops, is then used to secure a loan from a bank or from a venture capital firm.

Some of these same books go to great lengths describing the process of raising capital with a public offering of stock. Securities and Exchange Commission (SEC) regulations and prospectus formats are presented and embellished.

My complaint with all these books is not that their treatments are untrue or inaccurate. On the contrary, the material is usually substantive and factual. But it is also irrelevant and inapplicable to 9 out of 10 new business situations. Here's why:

- A business plan is important in securing a loan from a bank, but it is not sufficient. Substantial collateral and/or a proven track record are most often the ingredients that make loan officers sit up and take notice.

- Venture capital firms are not the least bit interested in *most* small business startups—franchisers, new retailers, catering businesses, new kitchen gadget inventors. Rather, these firms prefer to seek out specialized investment opportunities that may provide exceptional capital appreciation. Quite often, their interest focuses on ventures based on an emerging technology.

- Probably less than one in a thousand new businesses could successfully raise capital through a public stock offering. In fact, depressing as it sounds, most successful, long-established small businesses would not succeed with a public stock offering. Glamorous and high-technology ventures in two categories are most likely to succeed with a public offering.

THE REAL WORLD.

Bill Henry and Carl Hollins, both electrical engineers, several years ago discovered a need for a device that gives detailed, instantaneous printed information on the cost, time, and destination of local telephone calls. Most hotels charge a flat fee for local calls made from a guest room, but since they have no record of the length of calls or what zone they are made to they usually lose money on phone calls. The Henry and Hollins device is designed to give each guest a printout of calls and charges at checkout time, thereby, hopefully, increasing hotel's revenue from telephones.

Initial capital for product design and development—from their savings accounts and the cash value of their insurance policies— totalled about $30,000. Two systems have now been built and sold to local hotels. The partners feel that a market for at least 100 systems a year is easily attainable. But one problem stands in their way: capital to set up a manufacturing operation. "We're afraid to accept orders because we can't raise the needed capital. We've already raised an additional $20,000 by borrowing from friends, and I've taken a $15,000 second mortgage on my home," says Hollins, "but most of this went to pay bills. We should have gotten more money before we started, but we had no idea how fast we would spend it."

Henry and Hollins have explored just about every possible source of manufacturing capital. "Many bankers don't understand what we're doing. And if they do, they're concerned that a giant computer company will come in and steal our market. Then there are collateral requirements. We don't have much, only our lab equipment and electronic components. It's not worth much in the resale market.

"And venture capital companies aren't interested. We're too small, they say. And we don't have a track record. We've approached the SBA, but you have to have an 'in' or the red tape can bury you.

"We're going to try a private stock offering," says Henry, although he concedes that he has no specific investors in mind. "If this fails, we may have to sell out to a large, established manufacturer."

The *real world* for Henry and Hollins is much different from the idealized stuff described in many small business books. The real world told them that:

- Their initial capitalization was inadequate.
- Banks will not give them a loan because they lack a track record and collateral.
- Venture capital firms are not interested.
- The SBA route may take too long and may not be fruitful, anyway.
- A private stock offering is a shot in the dark at best.

Let's take a look at each of the realistic financing alternatives.

SELF-FINANCING.

One of the most repeated phases in the business and real estate community is "other people's money," or OPM. The philosophy behind OPM is that the easiest way to get rich is by using other people's money. For example, in real estate you buy a building for 10 percent down, borrowing 90 percent from a lending institution or from the seller. Assume that your down payment is $5,000 making the total purchase price $50,000, and that three years later you sell the building for $70,000. Your gain is $20,000 and you've multiplied your

$5,000 investment by 4. So your return, because you used OPM, is not $20,000 ÷ $50,000, or 40 percent but rather a whopping $20,000 ÷ $5,000, or 400 percent. OPM is probably the way to go if you can find the "other people," and if you can afford the cost of borrowing (which is tax deductible but highly expensive these days).

Let's go back to Bill Henry and Carl Hollins for a moment. Their case, which is not unusual, demonstrates that their only *reliable* source of financing was themselves. And their methods of self-financing are probably the most common ways to generate initial capital for a new small business:

Savings   Set aside a reserve for emergencies—at least 3 months' income. Then go ahead and invest as much of the remainder—or as much as you feel comfortable investing—in the business.

Second mortgage   With the rapid rise in residential real estate values, many people have equity in their homes that can be used to secure a second mortgage. But be aware that this mortgage is a lien against your home. You must make the monthly payments, or you could lose your residence.

Insurance   The cash value of whole life insurance can be a source of capital. Check with your insurance company concerning eligibility, interest rates, and terms.

Credit unions   Some employee credit unions grant personal loans. I know of one man who borrowed $8,000 from a company credit union under some pretext. But he used the money to invest (or gamble, depending on your view point) in the stock market. Obviously, he thought that he could make more in the market than his loan was costing him.

RELATIVES AND FRIENDS.

Relatives and friends are a good source of capital. They also happen to fall into the category of the "other people" in OPM. However, raising capital from personal acquaintances can create friction. It can even destroy relationships, if the worst happens.

There are actually two types of business financing. The first called debt financing, is simply borrowing at a predetermined interest rate.

The other approach, called equity financing, involves selling a portion of the ownership of the business. Public stock offerings are a form of equity financing.

Either type of business financing can be used with relatives and friends. Some potential sources of money might like to feel that they are simply loaning you money, while other sources might welcome the opportunity to get in on the action by buying shares or by becoming a minority partner. I know of a situation where a man raised about $50,000 by selling to friends and relatives about a 40 percent interest in his business. His largest investor bought $5,000 worth of stock, so nobody in the investment group was risking a great deal.

An interesting alternative to incorporating and selling stock is to set up a limited partnership and then sell shares to investor friends and relatives. Two sisters raised over $100,000 with this approach to begin a health food restaurant. A limited partnership must have at least one general partner who has unlimited liability. In the health food restaurant venture, the sister who had the least personal assets to risk became the general partner. The other sister had a home, so she assumed a limited partnership position, as did all of the other investors. This made all the investors (who, remember, were also the borrower's friends and relatives) more comfortable because each only risked as much as he or she invested.

BOOTSTRAP FINANCING.

Bootstrap financing takes its name from the old expression about pulling yourself up by your bootstraps.

In business, bootstrap financing means utilizing internal management capabilities to generate extra capital. It is management coaxing the business to function at a higher-than-normal level of financial efficiency. Let's look at each of the major contributors to bootstrap financing.

Accounts Receivable

Typically a large portion of a company's working capital is tied up in accounts receivable, that is, in products that have been sold and shipped but not yet paid for. Management attention is needed to convert these assets into usable cash efficiently.

Overly generous credit policies, created with the express purpose of generating goodwill and encouraging purchases, can result in too many slow-paying customers. It could also lead to excessive bad debt (accounts receivable written off as uncollectable).

A reasonable, yet firm, credit-granting policy must be established from Day 1 and then adhered to. New customers should not be granted much credit until they demonstrate their ability and desire to pay invoices when due.

Control and collection procedures are also essential. Large companies have full-time credit and collection managers to handle these tasks. You will not be so fortunate. Records indicating the condition of each customer's account should be updated and reviewed monthly. Accounts receivable should be analyzed in terms of days past-due. Accounts or payments that are 60 or 90 days past-due deserve special collection attention.

Don't hesitate to pursue past-due accounts aggressively. After all, your creditors will surely pursue you. You have every right to pursue your delinquent credit customers, tactfully but persistently. Books and chapters in financial handbooks are available where you can read about collection techniques. Instituting a finance charge on any amount past-due may be necessary. If this policy is implemented, be sure credit customers are aware of it when they make purchases.

Besides collecting from customers, there are two other ways to turn accounts receivable into cash. The first is to use the receivables to secure a bank loan. Typically banks will advance 50 percent to 80 percent of receivables' value when purchased goods are shipped. This system makes for a continuous line of credit as mature accounts are paid off and new shipments are borrowed against. Interest is calculated on the total of outstanding accounts.

The second technique involves the out-and-out sale of accounts receivable to a third party. This party, called a factor, assumes full responsibility for credit evaluation and collection. With factoring, your business essentially receives cash upon shipment while your customers are extended credit by the factor. Factoring companies purchase accounts receivable for their full value and advance 60 percent to 80 percent of their worth when goods are shipped. The factor assumes responsibility for bad debt. It pays the remainder of the receivable when due. A factoring agreement typically allows the factor to withhold payments only if the account does not pay because of faulty merchandise.

Factors typically cost more than accounts receivable loans. In addition to interest on advances, factoring companies charge 1 to 2 percent of each account's value as compensation for risk. But factoring can be arranged more simply and quickly than accounts receivable loans, and sometimes businesses which are not financially sound enough to qualify for bank financing can, and do, qualify with factoring companies.

Accounts Payable

Roles are reversed here. Instead of maximizing your efforts to collect or borrow against money owed the business by accounts payable, you want to optimize the use of credit you receive from suppliers.

A trade-off is typically involved. Suppliers often offer a cash discount for prompt payment (about 2 to 4 percent of the invoice value). You can extend your credit to 30, 60, or even 90 days by foregoing the discount and delaying payment. This option, however, is accompanied by the danger of a damaged credit rating, so good judgment must be exercised. Sometimes a request for delayed billing or a partial payment schedule can be arranged.

In one sense the credit associated with collecting from customers and extending payments to suppliers is a circular phenomenon. In times of cash shortages and tight credit, customers will try to use your credit longer, and, in time, you will be forced (because of a shortage of cash) to delay payments to your suppliers.

Progress Payments

Progress payments are another useful bootstrap financing tool. Customers pay for work as it is completed rather than after delivery. Examples of progress payments include:

- All down payments
- Payments collected by building contractors after each stage of construction is finished and inspected
- Deposit requests that accompany a custom order
- Raw materials furnished by customers, such as the paint used by an interior decorator

Inventory

It is all too common for businesses (both small and large) to have excessive capital tied up in their own inventories. Most businesses are well aware that it costs them 15 percent to 20 percent a year to carry inventory. This percentage includes interest expense, insurance, storage space expense, handling, and, sometimes, taxes.

But knowing the high cost of inventory and doing something to lower it seem to be two different things. I once did some consulting work for a small company whose finished goods' warehouse was overflowing, while, at the same time, many items were out of stock. Just about every day the sales staff put an emergency request to the manufacturing department to make another item that had just run out of stock. Inventory costs were running over 20 percent per year, yet the customers were not being serviced properly.

Good inventory management is not easy. But it is not overly complex, either. Readily understood, manual inventory control systems can be instituted in most businesses to free up working capital while maintaining or even improving customer deliveries. Consult suppliers and fellow businesspersons for guidance.

Equipment

Businesses can rent or lease just about anything nowadays. Consider this option for all equipment decisions. Quite often renting or leasing is more attractive than borrowing money to make a purchase. Leasing generally requires no down payment, while most new equipment loans require a down payment of 20 to 30 percent. The Bank of

America's *Small Business Reporter* has an entire booklet devoted to equipment leasing which is very instructive.

Another equipment option worth exploring is the *used* equipment option. There are companies in the business of selling all types of used equipment—from office furniture to production machinery. Sometimes these items are remanufactured to a condition almost like new, yet sell at half the original price or less.

Aggressive Marketing

If a company needed cash quickly, the best way to generate it may be through a special sale or other sales promotion vehicle. As I'm writing this, a major airline has just resumed service after a long and costly strike. The strike was so long, in fact, that the airline stopped taking reservations during the strike's duration. So upon resumption of operations, the airline faced the unhappy possibility of flying hundreds of almost empty planes. The airline opted for an aggressive marketing position. It offered half-fare round-trip coupons to anybody flying its planes during the first 3 weeks after service resumed. They even accepted tickets written by competing airlines. Customers eagerly took advantage of this offer.

Aggressive marketing techniques can help out in times of cash shortages. A promotion or special sale might also be a good time to weed out marginal products or reduce excessive inventories.

Cost-conscious Management

Every dollar saved by applying sound cost controls is a dollar saved in working capital. When a business is prospering, cost control is frequently lax. Expense accounts are not scrutinized. Purchases of extra supplies go unnoticed. New equipment is purchased without competitive bids.

Then suddenly, sales reach a plateau or the economy falters, and management tightens the cost control reins. New hiring is frozen. Only necessary business travel is authorized. Cost reduction programs are instituted.

Isn't there a better way? Why not a happy balance between being lax and being Scrooge-like. If costs are controlled reasonably well during good times, it may not be necessary to tighten the screws so much during bad times.

BANK FINANCING.

Contrary to the impression I may have given so far in this chapter, banks do give loans to small businesses, both for startup and for operations. But banks look for items in loan applications that many owners of new small businesses can't provide, such as:

- A solid personal credit record
- Ability to repay the loan
- Experience in the business he or she would like to enter

Banks are conservative. We like them to be that way when we open a savings account, so we must live with their philosophy when applying for a business loan. But remember, you have nothing to lose in applying for a loan. All it takes is your time. The Bank of America's *Small Business Reporter,* in its booklet *Financing Small Business,* goes into great detail on such topics as types of loans, loan applications, etc.

If you are fortunate enough to qualify for a bank loan, do one more thing—shop around. Remember that when you are borrowing money, you are actually *purchasing* the use of money, and the purchase price and repayment terms can vary considerably from institution to institution. I'd suggest calling at least six loan officers and filing applications at the two banks that offer the best deal.

Even if you don't qualify for a bank loan, bankers can be helpful. Often they are aware of private investors who are interested in capitalizing on new business ventures. Private investors are frequently willing to assume more risk than banks.

Don't overlook commercial finance companies when searching for a loan. But since most of these institutions rely on business collateral to secure loans, most of their loan activity is with ongoing businesses.

One other possibility is consumer finance companies. They offer personal loans in the $5,000 to $10,000 range and second mortgage loans above $10,000.

SMALL BUSINESS ADMINISTRATION.

Much has been written about the SBA and its small business loan programs. The details and requirements for qualifying for SBA loans can be found in many small business books in your local public library.

However, the failing of many of these books is that they make getting an SBA loan sound simple, when actually it is not at all simple. First, there is a good deal of paperwork involved, and when this is complete, there are often long waiting periods. And for many, there is a refusal. Although it hasn't been proved, many people have alleged that minorities living in the inner city have an easier time getting a loan than other applicants. Allegations have also been made that women now receive preferential treatment over men. I've appeared on several radio talk shows where listeners complained of reverse discrimination and told how they had experienced it themselves. One man said that an SBA loan officer told him that he would have gotten the loan that had been denied him if he were a woman.

Currently the SBA is in trouble with Congress, too. Several senators have publicly stated that they feel the SBA should be shut down because of mismanagement, kickback scandels, and the outrageous waste of taxpayers' money. So by the time you read this book, anything I say about the SBA may only be academic. Surely, however, there will be some improvements made at the SBA. So do file an application if you need a loan.

SMALL BUSINESS INVESTMENT COMPANIES.

Small Business Investment Companies (SBIC) and Minority Enterprise Small Business Investment Companies (MESBIC) are two other financing alternatives. SBICs and MESBICs are licensed by the SBA to supply capital to companies unable to raise funds from other sources. Both SBICs and MESCICs are privately owned, chartered by state laws, operating under SBA guidelines and penalties, and seeking profitable investments. They are usually willing to take greater risks than other capital sources, such as banks.

SELLING OUT.

Your financing problems may not be over once your business is established and growing. This is true because small businesses even in the $5 to $50 million sales range have difficulty raising capital to finance expansion. Venture capitalists are often not interested. Securities and Exchange Commission (SEC) regulations have made public stock offerings overly expensive, and underwriters shy away from small (and to them, often unprofitable) offerings. The SEC has just loosened up some of its regulations, but many experts question the value of these changes.

Sometimes the only option open to a small business in need of expansion capital is to sell out. Take the case of Halo Products. Halo was started about 17 years ago by John Mercer with a second mortgage on his home and loans from friends and relatives. It pioneered in the field of plastic wrappers and food storage bags. Its growth has been phenomenal. Its most recent annual report notes revenues of about $70 million and profits of almost $6 million.

Yet Halo had a problem. It needed capital to expand and to increase product research, but could not find it.

There was no alternative. Growth was essential to satisfy customer demand and to ward off competition. But money for growth was available only by selling out to a giant diversified firm. So Halo was sold. John Mercer is a millionaire several times over, but he no longer owns his own small business. Instead, he is an *independently wealthy* professional manager! Not bad. Not bad at all.

TEN

Enterprising women.

Everything in the other chapters of this book applies to women enterpreneurs as well as to men entrepreneurs. But I feel there is a need for a chapter specifically for women who are thinking about entering business, not because women need special help, but because of the way the world interacts with businesswomen.

Women entrepreneurs face special situations and special problems—situations and problems inherent in a world where women's equality is an objective we are working toward, rather than a reality.

WHY START A BUSINESS ANYWAY?

The topic of this section illustrates beautifully why this book needs a special chapter for women. Many women start businesses for reasons different from men's. And these unique reasons have an impact on the type of businesses selected and on the probability of success.

Women who are actively employed in the business community frequently feel that their careers are blocked, not because they lack experience or talent, but simply because they are the "wrong" sex. This is sad but true. Changing employers is sometimes the answer, but not always. Of course, this situation has improved in the last decade and will continue to improve, but hundreds of career women run into this unfortunate roadblock every year. For them, a viable option is to launch their own business.

Another major reason why women start their own businesses is because many do not qualify for a well-paying job in business or industry. This is especially true for women whose primary experience centers on raising a family and keeping house. It's also often true for women with years of experience in charitable work or community activities. Don't get me wrong. I'm not saying this is right, nor am I condoning it. I'm just saying that this is the way it is.

Sexist career blockage and the unwillingness of the business community to recognize the value of women's experience in traditional roles (e.g., wife, mother) motivate many women to enter the world of the self-employed. But other uniquely female motivators, such as the desire to work at home while raising small children, are also important.

What this all says is that women frequently enter their own business with a weak background and experience base. After all, when a woman is pigeonholed in a secretarial job for years, what chance does she have to gain experience in budgeting, hiring, and supervising? What chance does a mother who has raised three children have to sharpen her selling skills or learn cost accounting? I don't know of any relevant statistics, but my gut feeling is that women entrepreneurs experience a higher failure rate than do men entrepreneurs. I say this not because women have less ability, but because women starting business today matured in a world of sexual bias.

There are actions women can take to improve their odds for success. The first is to choose their business opportunities wisely. The message is clear: since women are starting off with an extra strike or two against them, they should select a business that accentuates their natural and acquired strengths and minimizes their weaknesses and limitations.

CHOOSING YOUR BUSINESS OPPORTUNITY.

After graduation from college, my first job was as an analytical design engineer for Pratt and Whitney Aircraft, the company that designs and manufactures most of the free world's jet aircraft engines. Pratt and Whitney had a huge engineering operation, with literally hundreds of analytical design engineers. We each had a gray metal desk in a huge, open office space. In this mass of humanity, one engineer stood out—Barbara Murphy. Barbara stood out because she was the only female engineer.

Barbara was hard-working and capable. But for some reason I could never fathom, she chose to work in an environment where her sex was a hindrance rather than an advantage. She was attractive, so she could never leave her desk without dozens of heads swiveling as she passed down the aisle. This upset her so much that she finally stopped using the main aisle. She was also very proper, so her presence at meetings meant that off-color remarks and four-letter words were dropped. The shop workers were tough for her to take, too. Whenever she went out into the factory, she was whistled at, stared at, and generally the focus of a good-natured commotion. It eventually got to such a point that she needed a male engineer as escort in order to feel comfortable enough to go out into the factory. Her job responsibilities required these forays at least once each day.

I have nothing against a woman being an engineer. I'm embarrassed to report how badly men treated Barbara at work. But that's the way it was. Barbara exhibited a great deal of courage. She stayed on at Pratt and Whitney for 4 years, but unfortunately she was never really accepted.

This may label me as chauvinistic, but I think Barbara would have been better off working for a company where being a female engineer was an asset, not a liability. Several possibilities come to mind. How about a position as an interior styling engineer for one of the auto makers? In a "man's world," people might sit up and take notice of a uniquely female contribution. Auto executives know how influential women are in the purchase decision for new cars. How about being an engineer for a cosmetics company, a food company, or a household appliance manufacturing company?

I think women have every right to compete in every facet of the business world. But a female engineer in a jet engine company is just beating her head against the proverbial brick wall.

This set of attitudes carries over into the way women select businesses for themselves. It seems to me that many women select businesses that put them at a disadvantage. I don't care how competent a woman is or how hard she tries, not many women are going to succeed in an auto body shop or as a plumbing contractor.

And on the other extreme, too many women gravitate to business opportunities that are traditionally female. Hairdressing, day care, secretarial services, and fashion boutiques are typical examples. In these situations, being female is not an advantage either. Rather, it is almost assumed that the proprietor is female. Probably more women enter traditional female businesses than any other.

For women who are a little more daring, I recommend another route. A third category of business opportunities for women are those where being female is an advantage. I like to encourage women to enter businesses in this category because it improves their chances of success.

Let me illustrate this category by pointing out that the most prosperous and the most successful hairdressrs are men, not women. Vidal Sassoon is a striking example. For some reason, women will pay more to have their hair done by a man than by a woman. Women hairdressers make a living, but men hairdressers make the bucks.

So why can't women play the same game when they enter business? Well, they can, and some of them do. I'm not aware of any barbershops owned and operated by women, but I'm sure they would prosper. And I'm not talking about fronts for massage parlors. I'm talking about legitimate barbershops. I'd rather have my hair cut by a woman simply because I think women have a better sense of what length and style of cut looks good on a man.

One business where women are doing very well by taking advantage of their gender is the industrial selling business. Some of these women are salaried salespersons and others are manufacturers' representatives. In either case, the fact that most industrial sales personnel are male is contributing to women's success. Surveys have found that compared with men, women salespersons are turned down less frequently when requesting an appointment, spend less time waiting in lobbies, close sales more frequently, and produce larger average orders.

Sure, women salespersons are vulnerable to sexual harassment and sexual overtures. But the good ones rise above these obstacles. Their capabilities as salespersons and the knowledge of the product are what makes them successful.

Other business opportunity areas where being a female is an advantage include industrial telephone surveys, real estate sales, and many others. I know of a woman who was working to help her husband ease the college tuition burden of their eight children. One evening she realized that her college-going daughters were studying everything but one of the most important roles they'd ever fulfill—mothering.

The woman pursued her idea. She felt there was a need for motherhood training *by* mothers. Eventually she received a government grant to fund her courses at a local university. The money paid a salary for her and several assistants.

Pursuing a "being-female-is-an-advantage" new business takes extra effort and determination. But the results are often worth it. I'd suggest that you seek out business opportunities that take advantage of the fact that women are a minority in the business community. As of now, women own less than 5 percent of the businesses in this country. Picking a business that maximizes your chances of success will help improve this sorry statistic.

PERSONAL RELATIONSHIPS.

Women entrepreneurs frequently experience difficulties in the personal relations area when they enter their own business. This is no doubt true because a woman starting a business is doing something that is generally considered out of the ordinary, and this can cause friction in personal relationships.

The most obvious area of difficulty is between a wife and husband. Some men still get upset and threatened when their spouse brings up the subject of working. Just think how these same husbands react when their wives start or purchase their own business.

Not all husbands are like this. Many would love to have their wives succeed in business. They are open to change and they don't feel threatened. But if your husband is in the first category, I'd suggest that you talk it over. Tell him about your plans and aspirations, your motives, and—especially—your feelings. Quite often, a series of conversations over a period of time will be needed. These talks will surely help with his understanding and they may even win his support.

Another set of relationships that are often upset when a woman enters business are those with close female friends. They may secretly resent your initiative, your creativity, and your energy. You'll be better prepared to cope with this phenomenon if you anticipate it. Frequently, the crisis passes when your friends realize that you are still the same person you've always been.

BUSINESS RELATIONSHIPS.

Unfortunately, women entrepreneurs have found that they have difficulty in some business relationships solely because they are women. For example:

- An irate customer may say something like, "May I speak to the boss?" or "Can I please talk to the owner?"
- Contractors may not live up to their promises and commitments because they figure that they can get away with it with a woman.
- Suppliers may not initially provide the same quality of service that they would for a man in the same situation.
- Banks may not process your loan application unless it is signed by your husband.

I could go on and on but I'm sure you get the idea. Succeeding in a business is not easy. Succeeding in a business as a woman is even more of a challenge.

Thankfully, your business relationships will improve with time, once people get to know who you are and what you can do.

MAKING THE TRANSITION.

Many women initially start businesses in the home, especially when their children are small. This is fine. In fact, as I've noted earlier, it's one of the best ways to start a business because it minimizes overhead and risk.

But there comes a time in the development of an at-home business when it's necesary to make the transition to a location out of the home. This is true for emotional as well as for business reasons.

Operating your business from a separate location will increase your stature and credibility as a businessperson. It will also establish you in the eyes of your children and husband as a businessperson as well as a mother and wife.

Businesswomen have found that establishing a separate identity in the eyes of family is almost impossible when the business is located in the home. There are all those scraped elbows and requests for Kool Aid to contend with.

Men can contend more successfully with an at-home business because they aren't expected to run the household at the same time they run the business. It's also sometimes easier because men are conventionally viewed as the breadwinners, even if they work at home.

TAKING ADVICE AND USING IT.

I can't write this section without mentioning a woman I wrote about in an earlier book of mine, *How to Pick the Right Small Business Opportunity.*[1]

Her name is Elaine McGill. I think it's important to relate her story

---

[1]Kenneth J. Albert, *How to Pick the Right Small Business Opportunity,* McGraw-Hill, 1977.

because it so beautifully illustrates the point of this section. Elaine, at the age of 24, found herself with the sole responsibility for running the family's furniture and cedar flakeboard manufacturing business. Her father had died suddenly and tragically, leaving her with a business she knew nothing about. Indeed, she had no prior business experience. To make matters worse, the business was in the midst of a transition that, if handled improperly, could take it and the family right into bankruptcy.

Without firsthand knowledge, she had to rely heavily on the counsel of a group of advisers. This group included the company's sales manager and plant manager, as well as a lawyer, an accountant, and the management consulting firm I was associated with.

From the first, Elaine appeared confident and in absolute control. I remember a meeting attended by myself, the lawyer, and the accountant. The topic was a heady one—the future legal structure of the company. Elaine took charge. She asked probing questions. She encouraged everyone to speak freely, to support our own recommendations, and to challenge other opinions. I can tell you there was a lot of challenging. The lawyer, the accountant, and the consultant agreed on very little that day. But it didn't faze Elaine. At the close of the meeting she thanked everyone for their honest candor and announced that she would now be able to make the necessary decisions. And that is just what she did. As time passed, one good decision followed another.

Women in business should seek out good advice. It's not a sign of weakness, but of strength. Then, once the advice is given decisiveness is called for. It's your business. You will rise or fall with the decisions, so you must make them. This direction applies as much to businesswomen as to businessmen. As I illustrate in the next chapter, procrastination is a condition that all too often proves fatal.

WOMEN'S SUPPORT GROUPS.

The director of the American Women's Economic Development Corporation (AWED), the first federally funded organization to train women entrepreneurs, was recently quoted as saying, "Women have a tougher time than men. They're more isolated, they have less work experience, and they have no contacts."

To equip women with the management and technical tools needed for survival, this organization and others have been formed. AWED has set up a full-year, free training program for independent businesswomen. The program consists of three full-day weekend sessions during the first month and a half, then a 3-hour session each month for the rest of the year. These sessions are conducted by volunteer professors from leading business schools.

Another type of support group for women planning or currently operating a business is the National Association of Women Business Owners (NAWBO). NAWBO has a national headquarters (in Washington, D.C.) and local chapters in major metropolitan areas. Its purpose it to encourage and educate its members, and even to pass on some business to them. Local chapters typically hold monthly meetings featuring guest lecturers. Some chapters also have workshops and seminars on various small business issues. Directories of women-owned businesses are being developed.

Both AWED and NAWBO are in their infancy, but already they are providing invaluable support to women. No doubt they will expand and be joined by other groups in the future.

Women's support groups offer a good deal of assistance on the issues raised in this chapter. I strongly suggest that women reading this book get involved in organizations dedicated to the advancement of women who own businesses.

One word of caution: A recent *Wall Street Journal* front-page article headline announced, "Business Is Booming for Those Who Help Women In Business—A Lot of It is Gimmickry." Leaders in the female business community and in women's equality groups concur that too many programs are ripping women off. Be on guard. Ask for names of satisfied participants and follow up on them.

ELEVEN

How to overcome hazards and pitfalls.

Hazards and pitfalls are part of all aspects of life—including starting and managing a small business. And it is as true in business as it is in parenting or gardening or whatever, that hazards and pitfalls can be avoided by applying a measure of knowledge and foresight.

Of course, neither life nor small business can ever be totally safe. The purpose of this chapter is to explain how to overcome a broad range of small business hazards and pitfalls. Obviously, they all don't apply equally to each type of business. As you read this chapter, note those that could apply to your type of business and also note any questions or issues that come to mind. Then, if you do decide to proceed with a business of your own, you'll be on your way to identifying, addressing, and, hopefully, minimizing potential problem areas.

There is no significance to the sequence of the topics in this chapter. Except that I am going to lead off with a subject that I, and many other small business advisers, feel is by far the most common shortcoming of managers of unsuccessful or marginal small businesses.

FAILURE TO PLAN AND TO FOLLOW THROUGH.

Planning is something that is familiar to us all and something that most of us feel we are quite good at. Why, then, is it so frequently cited as a shortcoming of small business management?

Maybe it's because many of us are not as good at planning and following through as we think we are. Or possibly it's because of the reality gap between knowing and doing: *knowing* that smoking, being overweight, and not exercising are bad for us, but not *doing* anything to change our behavioral deficiencies.

Whatever the reason, the fact remains that planning and following through are critical to small business success. If you get no other message from this chapter, at least get that one.

Several years ago I was interested in having some major remodeling work done on my home. One of the contractors I called was the epitome of a poor business planner. To begin with, 2 weeks passed, and I made several follow-up phone calls to him before he even came out to my house to appraise the job. One Thursday, another 2 weeks later, he stopped by and said that his quote was now ready. In the conversation that followed he asked, "If you accept my quote, when could I start the job?" I responded, "As soon as you like, I guess." "Well, could I start next Monday?" he asked. "You see, my crew is finishing up a big job tomorrow so they will be available on Monday." Now this contractor was not thinking and planning ahead. He'd probably known for weeks approximately when the current job would run out. Yet he took a month to prepare and present my quote. If he didn't get a job from me or someone else in the next 2 days, his crew would be idle on Monday morning.

Unfortunately, this type of situation is all too common among small business managers. They're so busy dealing with day-to-day problems that they don't take time to plan ahead.

There is another message in the story of my contractor acquaintance. The message is that planning is not an esoteric or obscure exercise. Rather, planning is the essence of ongoing business management. Our contractor didn't have the next assignment ready for his crew because he didn't prepare quotations promptly. Planning, for him, should mean scheduling his time and activities more effectively.

Some planning activities involve long-term (1 to 5 years) strategies and commitments. Other activities focus on tomorrow or next week or next month. The good manager is always planning and thinking ahead. Sometimes ahead is next week, other times it's 5 years from now.

Small business books often mislead readers by focusing their discussion of planning on the formal *business plan.* This plan typically is divided into sections covering business objectives, organization structure, key people, future staffing plans, marketing plans, and sales and market share forecasts, then closes with a financial analysis and forecast. Actually this type of plan has limited uses. Its primary purpose is to attract financial backers. It is also useful as an analysis and learning exercise. But a one-shot or yearly business plan and effective business planning are two separate and distinct things.

Good planning begins by identifying specific objectives and problems. Often this is best accomplished by asking a series of open-minded questions like:

- What are my three biggest problems?
- What weaknesses do my competitors have that I can exploit?
- Where would I like my business to be a year from today?
- What changes are taking place in the environment of my business (government regulations, consumer trends, etc.) and what should I do to prepare for them?
- What new business opportunities should I be pursuing?

From this process, a series of specific—and I do mean specific—goals and problems will develop. Now the multistep planning cycle is put into action:

1. Pertinent information needed for analyzing the situation is gathered.

2. Alternatives for action are laid out.

3. Alternatives are analyzed using the information gathered and relevant business principles.

4. A plan and realistic timetable is developed.

5. Follow-up and revision (as needed) are repeated until the plan becomes reality.

The last step—follow-up and revision—is so keyed to successful planning that I've given it major billing (as follow-through) in the title of this section. Plans without follow-through are meaningless. Milestones (a technique of goal setting) and management by exception are just two popular labels used to emphasize the importance of follow-through in today's business situation. But labels aside, it's follow-through that gets the job done.

To be most effective, the planning process should be applied to all aspects of a business. This includes marketing and sales, manufacturing, finance, human resources, and facilities. The planning cycle time period could vary anywhere from 1 or 2 days to several years, depending on the planning topic itself. For example, my would-be contractor should be able to go through the whole planning process and solve his problem in an hour or two. His best solution, of course, is to set aside a specific time each week for new business development. Then his follow-through would simply involve seeing that he actually takes that time each week, until this process becomes second nature to him.

Many small business managers have found that, in fact, the only way they can do a good job of planning is to designate a special time for it. Some do it during nonbusiness hours (Saturday morning, every other Monday evening) so they can insure an uninterrupted work period. Regular scheduled follow-up sessions are also essential.

One last point: To assess accurately the progress you're making toward an objective, you'll need a responsive and accurate system for data collecting and reporting. For example, if your goal is to increase average gross margin by 10 percent in the next 6 months, you've got to have current and believable inputs.

TIME AND PRIORITIES.

A pitfall which is a second cousin to planning and follow-through concerns time managing and setting priorities.

My observations suggest that people are either very good or very poor time managers. There appears to be no middle ground.

A popular school of thought suggests that poor managers of time are that way because they haven't been taught how to set priorities and how to develop a schedule and stick to it. I'm sure there is some truth to this. But I maintain that more is involved. Time management is just common sense. Most of us have enough common sense to know which tasks are important and how to plan our days, weeks, or months in order to get the important things done. But a lot of us don't.

Small business owners have many diverse tasks that must be performed. All are important, but at times some are more important than others. Letting the recordkeeping tasks slide, for example, because an owner is too busy working with customers, will eventually take its toll. Yet this is the kind of thing many small business managers do.

However, I don't think they do it because they are poor managers of time. I think they do it because there is a natural tendency to spend time doing the things we enjoy and to avoid doing the things we dislike. Many small business owners get into trouble because they gravitate to the most enjoyable aspects of running a business.

The freedom of being one's own boss is precisely the freedom that can create this type of problem. For an employee, there is always a boss who makes sure we spend time on the high-priority tasks—whether we enjoy them or not. But the boss and the pushing is gone when we have our own business: no one to tell us what to do, but also, no one to force us to do the tedious, undesirable tasks that are part of all jobs—even being self-employed.

Motivate yourself to do the things that must be done. Then your conscience will allow you to enjoy to the utmost the tasks that are fun and fulfilling.

One approach that often helps get the less-exciting tasks done is to have others do them. You can delegate them to employees. What may seem routine and cumbersome to you might be new or interesting to someone else.

Another way to have others do tasks that you don't enjoy is to farm them out. There are service companies that specialize in all kinds of things—from bookkeeping to window washing to collecting accounts receivable. Of course, delegating work to employees or farming out tasks costs money, but getting tasks done well, and on time, may save you money in the long run.

INDECISIVENESS.

Small business owners face problems and make decisions every day. Most are routine, such as reprimanding a tardy employee or negotiating a price with a customer. These situations generally do not precipitate indecisiveness.

Rather, it's the tough problems that are often difficult to face. Usually, these problems creep up over some extended period of time and do not lend themselves to quick and easy solutions. Problems in this category include shortages of working capital, improper inventory, and ineffective advertising, among many possibilities.

It is difficult for many small business managers to face up to these tough problems. Yet the essence of management is making decisions—decisions that are either necessitated by tough problems or are required to exploit opportunities. As Peter Drucker wrote in his landmark book, *The Practice of Management,* "Whatever a manager does, he does through making decisions."[1]

It follows that a business's success and future prospects depend on its owner's ability to make sound, tough decisions. Or to put it

[1]Peter Drucker, *The Practice of Management,* Harper and Row, 1954.

another way, successful business owners get that way by confronting tough problems and solving them.

Effectively confronting tough problems requires a practical, logical, and realistic approach. In my years of confronting problems as a management consultant I have distilled out some basic "tough decision" principles that have helped me. The most relevant of these are presented below, along with amplifying comments where appropriate.

1. *Every problem is an opportunity in disguise.* The dread of confronting a tough problem or messy situation can be overcome by taking on a positive attitude. This does not mean that you should put your head in the clouds. Rather, it means that you recognize that when a problem is identified and overcome, things will be better. Profits will improve or sales will increase. Problems are the opportunity to make things better.

2. *Almost all business problems can be solved by applying a logical, step-by-step approach.* By using the steps outlined here and by using common sense, you can solve problems. I know this to be true. Once you've tried it (you already may be intuitively applying portions of the method) you'll know it's true.

3. *Unless a situation is reversible, don't make a hasty decision.*

4. *Recognize symptoms early, then face the problem head-on.* Recognizing the symptoms of a problem is usually not too difficult. It's coming to grips with them that's hard. But experience tells us that problems rarely solve themselves. Instead they often get worse with time. So procrastinators pay the price.

5. *Before you can solve a problem, you've got to define it.* This sounds simplistic, but it's not. Sure, some problems are easily defined. But take a problem like this, for example: Two symptoms of company X's problem are (1) excessive finished goods inventory and (2) high levels of back orders. In which of the following areas is the problem?

- Sales forecasting
- Production scheduling
- Order processing
- Shipping
- Something else

With the information at hand, it was impossible to tell. In such a situation, a good first step is to gather enough information to define the problem accurately. Sometimes defining the problem is more than half the battle.

If your business is organized in such a way you have partners or other key management personnel besides yourself, it's important to reach a consensus on the definition of a particular problem. Good communication should then be maintained throughout the remainder of the problem-solving process.

6. *Develop a plan of action with a tight but realistic schedule.* After problem definition, the problem-solving process follows these basic steps:

- Information gathering
- Analysis of alternative solutions
- Selection of corrective action
- Implementation

A schedule should be developed indicating specifically what work is expected in each of these steps, and when it is expected to be completed. Do this even if you are solving the problem entirely on your own. The schedule will help keep your efforts on track.

7. *Put priorities into your problem-solving efforts.* You won't be able to tackle all the problems at the same time. So rank your problems in order of importance and address those at the top of the list. Setting priorities is also useful while working on individual problems. Priorities will prevent you from getting bogged down. They help you to keep the big picture in mind.

8. *Pinpoint problem-solving responsibility.* If someone besides you has prime responsibility for solving an important problem, be sure they know what is expected of them. Then, if the process is going to take several weeks or months, be sure to review periodically the progress that is (or isn't) being made.

9. *Don't hesitate to take drastic action when drastic action is called for.* Solutions to some problems can't wait. If a decision is called for, make it to the best of your ability and then go on to other matters.

10. *Effective problem-solving depends on your ability to gather the right information.* Let's go back to the example mentioned in principle five, above. The right information (individual item inventory history, items frequently back ordered, accuracy of the sales forecast, time required for order processing, shipping schedule, delivery time, etc.) in this and other situations allows the problem to be pinpointed accurately, and then solved. Initial information gathering should concentrate on developing an understanding of the present situation.

11. *People (and the written information they possess) are the main contributors to the information-gathering effort.* Gathering relevant information properly and expediently is probably the most critical and the most difficult task to master in problem solving. People who have the needed information may be peers or subordinates within your organization, or they may be people outside the organization, such as suppliers, lawyers, bankers, customers, or even competitors. Space does not permit me to do justice to this topic. I suggest you refer to my earlier books. Each covers important aspects of information-gathering through people. They are listed in the front matter.

12. *When appropriate, rely on best estimates, good judgment, and reasonable assumptions.* There is no such thing as perfect information. At best, facts are distorted by a lack of accuracy. And often nonfactual information (such as opinions or subjective forecasts) are more important than the most accurate facts.

13. *Begin formulating alternative solutions early in the information gathering process.* Early development of alternatives will help guide the processes of information gathering and analysis. Quite possibly, a newly formulated alternative will require that separate or additional information be gathered for analyzing and evaluating the alternative's merits. Another point: You can never develop too many alternative solutions. Poor solutions are easily discarded, but the best solution may never surface if it isn't first conceived as an alternative.

14. *Analysis means using information to draw sound conclusions, and then properly applying them to alternative solutions.* A meaningful analysis is based on these axioms:

- Always try to quantify your analysis, even in subjective or qualitative situations.

- Avoid analysis paralysis. Analyzing a problem to death accomplishes nothing.

- Pragmatism is essential. Don't seek the perfect solution. It probably doesn't exist.

15. *Carefully weigh alternatives to isolate a practical and timely solution.* Test your solution using "what if" questions. Remember, if your solution conflicts with common sense, find another solution. All good solutions take into account an organization's ability and motivation to implement it.

16. *A decision not to decide could be the best solution.* Sometimes, not frequently but sometimes, inaction is better then action. If you've conscientiously executed the fundamental problem-solving steps and have concluded that you should do nothing—fine. That's your solution.

17. *Always formulate contingency solutions for big problems.* Then if the situation changes or competition counters your moves, you'll be ready.

18. *Don't try to impose your solution on others.* Sure you're the boss and it's your business, but good managers make their employees feel that they are working *with* the boss and not *for* the boss. This leadership philosophy is appropriate to all aspects of management, including implementing solutions to tough problems. The best way to ensure that key people will be supportive is to encourage their involvement throughout the entire problem-solving process. Seek their advice and opinions. Bounce possible solutions off them early in the effort.

19. *Whenever possible use a small-scale test to evaluate the chosen solution.* This strategy prevents big mistakes. It's appropriate for anything from testing a new promotion to taking on part-time summer help to solve a staffing problem.

20. *If your solution impacts on people's jobs, tell them confidentially and quickly.* It's always difficult to give employees unpleasant news—that they are being let go, that their job responsibilities are being changed, or that they are no longer reporting to you directly but rather to your assistant. They're going to find out sooner or later, and it's better they find out from you than from the grape vine. Rumors are usually worse (and cause more anxiety) than the truth, anyway.

21. *Good implementation is a most difficult and hazardous task; treat it as such.* Finding the solution to a problem often is only the beginning of the battle. Putting a solution into effect takes patience and perseverance.

22. *Create and adhere to an implementation schedule.* This schedule, or work plan for implementation, should delineate each major step, when it is to be accomplished, and who is responsible for its accomplishment.

23. *Stick with a solution you believe in.* As I noted above, implementation of a solution for a tough problem is often difficult. Roadblocks will spring up. Some employees may begin to second-guess your judgment. But if you feel that the solution you have chosen is the best solution, hang in there.

24. *Set a realistic time for results to materialize, then see that they do.* Frequent, regular monitoring of progress is the only way to insure that implementation is working. Frequent status checks allow you to fine-tune or modify actions so that good results are attained.

25. *If you need an expert for some aspect of the problem-solving process, get an expert.* You're probably expecting a dictum like this from someone with a management consulting background. But, honestly, I'm saying it not because of preconceived notions, but because I believe it. Lawyers and accountants are essential in some situations, and so are marketing or distribution experts, store layout specialists, or export consultants.

26. *Careful planning and control will prevent many tough problems from ever developing.* Effective owners of small businesses spend most of their time planning and controlling, rather than solving tough problems. If brush fires and tough problems are consuming most of an owner's time, something is seriously wrong.

SERVING MANY MASTERS.

As employees, we all know what it's like to serve one master—our boss. Sometimes bosses can be frustrating, but usually, employees at least get to know what to expect from their bosses. This predictability and consistency makes most jobs tolerable, if not enjoyable.

But the transition from employee to small business owner is difficult for many. Part of the reason for this is that instead of having one boss and one set of expectations, self-employed people have many "bosses." Too many new business owners, once they break free of the corporate hierarchy, expect to escape the demands placed upon them by their superiors. They are shocked and disappointed to find that the bosses are replaced by half-a-dozen or more "bosses," including:

- Customers
- Suppliers
- Bankers (or other creditors)
- Landlords
- Employees

- Internal Revenue Service
- Community groups and organizations

Now, don't misunderstand me. I'm not saying that running a small business doesn't offer a great deal of freedom and independence. It does. But I'm saying it's important to recognize from the start that self-employment carries with it certain responsibilities and demands. Sure, they're diffrent from those that go with a job in a big company. But they do exist. The good manager of a small business recognizes the opportunities and satisfactions associated with these relationships and gains strength from them.

CRIME.

Many small business books avoid the burglary, robbery, and shoplifting issue for fear that it is not the kind of thing that the potential book buyer wants to read about. It's too negative and too frightening.

Other small business books include a limited amount of extremely basic information on burglary, robbery, and shoplifting. Some of this information is so basic and so simplistic that it can give the reader a false sense of confidence.

Every type of business is susceptible to losses due to crime. The degree of risk and the potential loss varies greatly by specific business activity and location. If you contemplate starting or purchasing a business, you should expect to spend some money for burglary, robbery, and possibly shoplifting protection.

But, rather than relying on the information put forth in books and pamphlets, I'd suggest you evaluate your particular situation by contacting your local police department and managers of local businesses. After talking with them, it may or may not also be necessary to contact locksmiths, alarm company representatives, insurance agents, and security consultants.

In few cases is the threat of crime pervasive enough to prevent one from going into business. But the possibility of burglary, robbery, and shoplifting should not be ignored.

BAD CHECKS AND BAD PLASTIC.

Another hazard you'll face, besides burglary and robbery, is associated with accepting payment in the form of checks and credit cards.

A simple way to avoid this problem if to run a cash-only business. But in our convenience- and credit-oriented society, businesses that do not accept checks and/or credit cards operate at a competitive disadvantage.

Again, this is a topic that is either not treated or is treated simplistically by most small business books. This is unfortunate because some retailers indicate that over 90 percent of their volume is in personal checks and credit cards.

Some knowledge and some decisions will be required on your part. You'll need to find out enough about this hazard (in your particular situation) to decide:

- An appropriate customer identification policy
- Procedures to educate your employees to spot bad checks and credit cards
- Whether to accept out-of-state checks
- Collection policy for bad checks
- Deterrents to set up, if any

A basic yet thorough overview of the entire crime prevention topic is available in the Bank of America's *Small Business Reporter* booklet entitled *Crime Prevention in Small Business*. Read this publication as a first step. Then delve into the topics where you have particular needs through personal discussions with experienced businesspersons.

EMPLOYEE THEFT.

A final crime-related topic is employee theft. (This subject is also treated in the *Small Business Reporter* mentioned above.) In many business situations, emppoyee theft results in more losses than any other form of crime. Government figures indicate that substantially more retail shortages are caused by employees than by shoplifters. In manufacturing and distribution companies, employee theft is the major threat of loss, well outdistancing burglary.

Of course, the other aspects of employee theft that make it so difficult to cope with is the diverse and concealed nature of the crimes. The variety of employee theft is limited only by the imagination of the perpetrators. And since the thefts are most frequently interwoven with the employee's job responsibilities, they are most difficult to detect.

The primary message that I want to convey concerning employee theft is that a business owner cannot trust his or her employees. I know this sounds harsh. But that's the way it is. One survey of employee-criminals concluded that the typical offender is highly regarded by his employer, has been on the job for an average of 5 to 10 years, and was not apprehended until years after the criminal behavior began. I'm not saying that you should be paranoid, but be cautious. Be careful. Institute systems that have checks and balances. And temper your faith in mankind with sound business judgments.

BRIBES, KICKBACKS, AND CASH SKIMMING.

Now that we've talked about everybody else's crime, it's only fair that we discuss some crimes of small business owners themselves.

Recently a big city newspaper went into the tavern business. Their purpose was to investigate corruption among city employees and small business owners. Two undercover reporters leased a defunct tavern and announced plans to refurbish and reopen it. During this process the following took place:

- A city building inspector took a bribe to overlook numerous code violations.
- The health inspector, his palm greased with a ten spot, issued a license despite roaches, filth, etc.
- Ditto for the fire inspector.

- A distributor of electronic games insisted on a kickback.
- A veteran bookkeeper and small business advisor, hired by the new tavern owners, suggested, "Keep two sets of books. Everybody who has a cash business does it. One is for actual cash receipts and one is for tax purposes."

For the uninitiated, this last item is called cash skimming. A blatant example of this technique just hit the national news when the owners of a famous discotheque in New York were indicted for skimming thousands of dollars a day from this lucrative cash-only business.

I'm sure that these examples of illegal practices are not isolated cases. These kinds of things go on every day in every part of the country. I'm not going to make an ethical or moral statement about them. I just want to make sure that you know that they exist. You can resist them or you can go along with them. Just as you can resist or go along with slipping a 10-dollar bill to the next cop who stops you for a traffic violation. It's your life and your business. You've got to run them the way you see fit.

FRAUD.

Fraud is a hazard that can dash your dreams of success and separate you from your startup capital before you know what happened. Worm farms are a beautiful example.

Common earthworms have become increasingly popular with farmers (to loosen soil) and for use in eliminating solid waste. But promoters have greatly exagerated the demand for worms to enhance their fraudulent schemes.

In advertising, seminars, films, and slide shows these promoters emphasize that the more money a worm farmer invests, the more he will earn at a later date. High-pressure selling has convinced many naïve buyers that the road to riches is through worm farming. A Securities and Exchange Commission investigator says that investors often purchase 2-foot-square boxes of 10,000 worms, paying $400 to $800 for worms that in many cases have a true market value of less than $50.

The big problem, the SEC says, is that the seller promises to buy back all the worms later, but actually has no intention of doing so. And marketing the worms by the investors themselves is a difficult if not impossible task, even if he or she is willing to take a loss. The SEC added that investors are not always told the truth about how rapidly worms reproduce, their true value, and the time and knowledge needed to raise them.

Personally, I can't believe that people are so gullible. But, they are. The problem is apparently nationwide. Authorities have issued cease-and-desist orders or filed suits against unscrupulous worm dealers in 17 states.

Of course, this is just one example. There are dozens of con games and fraudulent schemes. New ones are conceived each day. So keep your guard up.

RIGIDITY.

Successfully running a business takes flexibility and the ability to adapt to changing situations and roles. A small business, in this respect, is just the opposite of a large corporation. Managers in big companies typically are responsible for specialized functions, and often for narrow aspects within a function. But the multiple responsibilities associated with running a small business require the ability to move from area to area with ease and efficiency. You don't have to be equally proficient in each task, but you need to address responsibilities in each and see that they are fulfilled.

Excessive rigidity also creates problems as a business moves from the startup phase, through the established entity phase, to the growth phase. As a business grows and matures, the owner's responsibilities change from operating to planning, delegating, and controlling. By continuing to expand their management knowledge and executive skills, most small business owners are able to develop the flexibility to make this transition.

TWELVE

Lawyers, accountants, insurance agents, and other advisers.

It's possible to start and run a business without any outside advice. You can buy a book that will show you how to incorporate yourself (that is, if you choose to incorporate). You can set up and handle your own accounting function (or you can purchase ready-made recordkeeping systems). You can bear the risks associated with fire, theft, etc., yourself (it's called self-insurance). And you can make all your other key decisions without professional advice.

You know what? Too many persons operate new small businesses in this manner. Some do it to save money. Some do it because they don't want to admit they need help. And others do it because they don't know where to look for services and/or advice. Then there are the businesspersons who sincerely believe that they don't need anyone but themselves.

In my way of thinking, none of these reasons makes sense. No man is an island. And no businessperson is either. We all have strengths *and* weaknesses. We all know a great deal about some things and very little about other things.

Then there are the new small business owners who go overboard with lawyers, accountants, insurance agents, consultants, etc. They gloat over having an entourage of advisors. They spend too much time and too much money on these activities. Some people in this category unfortunately are afraid to make their own decisions, so they hire others to make them.

The purpose of this chapter is to help you utilize advisors to your best advantage, not by shunning them or overusing them, but by optimizing their benefits to you.

DETERMINE YOUR NEEDS.

Lawyers, accountants, and insurance agents, quite naturally, prefer you to rely heavily on the services they provide. That's not to say that most of them are unscrupulous, but let's face it, they're in business to make money. But so are you. So a good first step in buying professional services is for you to determine your needs. Then you can avoid overbuying.

Let's take a look at each major type of professional service and the most typical needs of a small business.

Some small businesses have a lawyer on a yearly retainer, but this appears to be atypical. More likely, established small business owners use lawyers on a selective basis. One veteran businessman who ran a thriving equipment rental business told me, "I use lawyers only for major stuff. To change a partnership agreement, or something like that. I handle my small claims myself. Up to $500. I detest lawyers. All they do is scare you."

But another successful entrepreneur (who has built a multimillion-dollar temporary industrial help business) cautions new businesspersons: "Don't hesitate to ask your lawyer for advice. You don't have to take it if you don't want to." Most small business people agree that you need a lawyer when starting out—for legal structure decisions, for negotiating if you're buying a business or taking on a lease, and for reviewing contracts.

Then, once you've past the startup phase, legal services should be needed only for special circumstances. A TV repair service owner told me, "I only use a lawyer when necessary. I needed one when I started but not on a sustaining basis."

Accountants present a somewhat more individualized situation.

Some small business people are capable of handling accounting functions themselves, including tax returns. Some small businesses require only the most elementary accounting and tax systems, so these can be handled in-house. But for most of us, bookkeeping, balance sheets, and tax returns are too specialized. If you're in this category, use professional assistance. It's surprisingly inexpensive. I know of one very good accounting service that has an average fee schedule for small businesses as follows:

- Setting up books: $100 to 300 (average $200)
- Monthly bookkeeping charge: $100
- Federal tax return: $100 to 200 (average $150)

So, an average year's total cost might be about $1,500 ($200 + [12 times $100] + $150). It sounds like a lot of money and it is. But by having it done *right* you might easily be way ahead. Without an accurate and informative set of financial data you can't tell where you've been or where you're headed.

Now for insurance: Almost everybody has auto insurance, health and life insurance, and home or renter's insurance. But for some mysterious reason, all too many budding entrepreneurs operate without any insurance to protect their assets from fire, water damage, theft, disability, liability, etc. To me, this is ridiculous. Begin by reading up on the various types of insurance. Many small business books (especially the voluminous ones) have a paragraph or two on each of the dozen or so types of coverage. The SBA also has some information pamphlets. Then meet with at least three insurance agents and pump them for all the information you can. Your time will be well spent. One last, but very fruitful, way to determine your insurance needs is to talk to experienced business owners. They know that business insurance is a necessary evil. As one owner put it, "Insurance is one undesirable thing that you have to buy."

One last note on professional service costs. There is some consolation in knowing that money spent on lawyers, accountants, and insurance (as well as on other professional counsel) is most often directly deductible from gross income. So these expense items will lower your income tax bite.

DON'T BE INTIMIDATED.

Once you have some idea what your needs are in the professional service area, the process of selecting and working with these people begins.

Some of the advice that's headlined in the titles of this and the following section is almost self-explanatory. That's the case with the title of this section: don't be intimidated. Not much more can be said, except that it's easier for me to say that you shouldn't be intimidated by lawyers and accountants, etc., than it is for you *not* to be intimidated.

I've found that it helps me to remind myself once in a while that I am the boss. The lawyer, the accountant, or the insurance agent is working for me. I'm paying them, not the other way around. These people may be experts, but they're working for me. When you hire one of them, then you'll be the boss. Say, for example, you want a meeting with your lawyer on Tuesday morning, and he says that Tuesday afternoon would be better. You say you can't make it in the afternoon and I'll bet he'll agree to the morning. If you behave like the boss, you'll be treated like the boss. You don't have to be unpleasant or demanding, just assertive.

USE SMALL BUSINESS SPECIALISTS.

Experienced small business people have found that they get the best service from lawyers, accountants, insurance agents, and other counselors who either specialize in working with smaller clients or at least do a high percentage of their work with small businesses. These people typically have more knowledge and experience in the special needs and requirements of small businesses. Also, since their livelihood depends on small clients, they tend to provide better service than a person who realizes most of his or her income from other sources.

Fortunately, it's easy to find these small business specialists. Every community has them. The way to find them is to ask three or four established small business owners in your area.

If you live in a large metropolitan area, try to stick with professional service people whose business activity is centered in the area you expect to operate in. They will then have first-hand knowledge of local situations and will be more accessible when you need them.

FIND OUT IN ADVANCE.

I recently concluded a real estate transaction. My relationship with my lawyer illustrates to a T the message of this section. He quoted me a fixed fee to handle the deal, which at the beginning appeared to be a simple, uncomplicated transaction. But even before the first papers were signed, things began to get messy. I asked my lawyer, John, if this would affect the fee. He said no. As the deal dragged on and got more and more messy, John didn't mention any fee change and I didn't ask. But after the deal closed John sent me a very pleasant letter saying, "As you recall, I indicated that my fee would be fixed unless the file becomes extraordinary. I feel you and I both agree that this file was extraordinary, Hence, the separate bill enclosed."

The separate bill was for a 45% increase over the original fixed quotation. I honestly don't recall John adding the qualification "Unless the file becomes extraordinary" to his original quote.

Now I face a dilemma. I don't feel obligated to pay John any more than the original fixed fee. Yet, because he did do a good deal of extra work, and good work at that, I feel he deserves more compensation. I'll probably end up paying John his extra 45%, but I could have avoided this problem by communicating better with John during the time we were working on the deal. Or he could have avoided the problem by saying something like, "Ken, this thing has gotten out of hand. I'm going to have to increase my fee."

It's good to find out in advance exactly what fee you will be asked for on any professional services you purchase. And this should be in writing, of course.

AVOID WISHY-WASHY ADVISERS.

I once did a management consulting assignment for a client who had the most wishy-washy group of advisers I have ever encountered. They never made recommendations, and it was impossible to pin them down. The lawyer was always talking about the implications of this or that alternative. The accountant could talk for hours (or at least that's how long it seemed) about this or that ramification.

Now discussing the issues is great. But you'll need advisers who can say, "I think you ought to do this for these reasons" or "If I were you I'd . . . ." They may not always be right, but at least you would know where they stand.

SOMETIMES GET A SECOND OPINION.

If a critically important decision is not clear-cut, it is sometimes worth it to get a second opinion. After all, Blue Cross is now experimenting with a second-opinion program for surgery cases. Good doctors don't mind. And neither do good professionals who provide service to small businesses.

Sometimes you can get a second opinion without the first adviser knowing about it. This prevents hurt feelings and the possibility of disturbing a good working relationship. I did just that very thing on the real estate deal I just described above. John gave me an opinion at a critical juncture in the negotiations. Not knowing much about law, I felt a need to confirm what John had said. After all, it was my money and my property at stake, not his. Happily, I had a friend who knew a good real estate lawyer. I called him, described the situation, and asked for a judgment off the top of his head. It agreed perfectly with what John had told me, so I felt much better.

Don't hesitate to get a second opinion when you feel the need, even if you have to pay extra for it.

DON'T BE AFRAID TO SWITCH.

Lawyers, accountants, insurance agents, and other advisers should not be considered permanent business fixtures. Especially in the early life of a business. It's always easiest to stick with the same person, but it's not always best for your business.

Often, as a business matures the company lawyer and the company accountant become board members. By this time you should know them and their work well enough to feel comfortable with that type of relationship.

ONE OTHER SOURCE OF ADVICE.

Currently, the federal government, through the SBA, is funding a program that many fledgling businesses are finding to be most helpful. It's called the Small Business Development Center program, and it's fashioned after the partnership established over a century ago by agriculture schools, the federal government, and the farmer.

Each center is associated with a business school and is staffed by a full-time director and assistant director, business school professors, and M.B.A. students. These centers provide professional help at no charge to business owners. They do everything from setting up recordkeeping systems to developing marketing plans, and even assisting in securing loans. The typical client of a Small Business Development Center has gross sales of less than $1 million, employs few people, and cannot afford professional consultants.

In addition to traditional counseling functions, each center specializes in problems faced by its particular small business environment. For example, the center at the University of Maine focuses on improving the state's timber industry, and the center in Florida has special concerns with the tourist industry.

Quite frankly, at first I was somewhat doubtful about the value of this program. Could college professors and college students actually help business people who face real world problems? Testimonials have convinced me that the answer is yes. These centers do help. I know of too many cases of productive relationships between the centers and small business people to doubt their contribution.

Small Business Development Centers are currently located at the following universities:

- California State University at Chico
- California State Polytechnic University in Pomona
- University of West Florida—Pensicola
- University of Georgia—Athens
- University of Maine—Portland
- University of Missouri—St. Louis
- Rutgers University—Newark
- University of Nebraska—Omaha
- Howard University, Washington, D.C.

Centers can be contacted directly. They welcome telephone inquiries.

THIRTEEN

Recordkeeping, regulations, and taxes.

Many small business books devote a great deal of space to record keeping, regulations, taxes, and other related topics. In theory, this is good. These are important topics. The more information available, the better.

But in several respects, these books do a disservice to the reader. Here's how:

- Authors of books on small business too frequently suggest or even state that all you need to know "is in my book. Buy it, read it, then do as I say and you'll have no worries or problems."

- Material is often presented so as to give the impression that readers must master all aspects of every topic, or they will surely join the ranks of people whose businesses have failed.

- Quite understandably, some readers are so overwhelmed by the apparent complexity of recordkeeping, regulations, and tax dissertations that they are scared away from the dream of owning their own business.

But successful small business people—as well as accountants, lawyers and tax specialists—counter the above erroneous notions with these insights:

- No book can tell you all you need to know; these topics are too involved. Anyway, the individual circumstances of *each* particular business cannot be treated in a book.

- These topics are so involved and so specialized that no businessperson ever masters them completely. Familiarity—yes; a working knowledge in some aspects—maybe; but mastery— never. There are thousands of successful small business people who couldn't file an accurate tax return if they had a whole year to work on it and nothing else.

- Federal, state, and local regulations fill volumes. Knowing how to cope with them, rather than learning all about them, is what a small business person has to master.

Now that I got that off my chest, let me tell you what this chapter is all about. I'm going to detail some basic (yet often overlooked) material that you should be familiar with. Also included will be sources of additional information, as appropriate. But, most importantly, the goal of this chapter is to help you set management priorities and avoid management pitfalls when dealing with recordkeeping, regulations, and tax-related topics.

ACCOUNTING AND RECORDKEEPING.

In the last chapter I strongly suggested that the best way to ensure having a useful and accurate accounting and recordkeeping system is to hire a good accountant or accounting service.

Of course hiring a specialist does not allow the small business owner to abdicate his or her management responsibility. The accountant will develop a system to satisfy your needs and expectations. So you'll need to establish objectives. Here's a good starter list:

- The system should portray results of all major operations clearly, quickly, and with full explanation.

- It should provide easy comparison of current figures with figures from other periods (last week, last month, last quarter, last year).

- A meaningful system should alert the business owner of problem areas. Is margin slipping? Are inventories growing excessively? Is accounts receivable in trouble? A good system will give you these answers and more.

- The accounting and recordkeeping system should also highlight problems in nonfinancial areas, such as spoilage, damaged merchandise, employee performance, theft, etc.

- It will allow for filing of accurate forms and tax returns.

- It should assist in the management decision-making process. Good decisions are based on good information. If, for example, the system provides net margin data by product, by sales territory, or by month, the owner can make marketing decisions aimed at maximum profitability.

How Much Is Enough?

There is no way I can tell you how detailed your recordkeeping system should be. That depends on your particular operation and its needs. But I can say that based on my experience with small business owners (and based on the experience of accountants who deal exclusively with small businesses), the typical small business has inadequate records. Also, surveys have correlated the adequacy of recordkeeping systems with the success of individual businesses. Almost half of marginal or failed businesses had poor records, while the vast majority of thriving small businesses had accurate and thorough records.

My advice is that if you're going to err concerning your system's sophistication level, err on the side of too much rather than too little. You can always weed out and simplify as you gain insight and experience.

Another how-much question concerns the business owner's need for advice and counseling. Having good information is one thing. But understanding what it tells you is quite something else. One popular way to interpret financial information is by the use of ratios, such as the current ratio and the acid-test ratio. Actually, there are dozens of ratios that can be calculated for interpretation. A quick course on this process is included in some small business books, but I wouldn't take such a course if I were you. I've taken sophisticated, graduate-level courses that included ratio analysis, and do you know what? I still don't feel confident or comfortable about any of it. And I don't think that many other self-employed people do, either.

Accountants who deal extensively with small business people sense that their clients are frequently reluctant to ask for advice and counsel. The business owner spends $100 or so a month for accounting services, and he expects the numbers by themselves to tell him what he needs to know. But, the business owner is frequently ill-equipped to interpret data. Rather than asking what it means, the owner shrugs and goes on to other things. Small business owners don't ask their accounting service for advice and interpretation because they know they will have to pay extra for it. This is foolhardy. Spend a little extra once in a while (a CPA's time might cost $20 to $70 per hour) to gain some insight. And don't blame the accountant for wanting to charge extra for it. As a friend of mine who is an accountant says, "You remind those small business owners that our inventory *is* time so we must charge for it."

Packaged Accounting Systems

Packaged accounting systems offer a low-cost alternative to the use of a professional accounting service or a CPA. These systems are widely available through office supply stores and from specific trade associations. (See SBA Small Business Biography Number 15 and SBA Small Marketing Aids Number 126, for example.)

There is a great deal of disagreement on the merits of packaged systems. Accountants, quite naturally, label them inadequate, saying that they don't allow for accrual or for development of a balance sheet. These accusations may or may not be true, depending on the system. However, developers and trade associations strongly defend these systems, when they are applied properly and conscientiously.

Personally, I don't think the saving associated with these systems is worth it. First, any do-it-yourself system takes time—time that probably would be better spent operating and managing the business. Second, by doing it internally, the business owner misses the opportunity for the second opinion and expert perspective of an accounting professional.

My advice is to check with business owners in your field. Find out what approach they're using and which they used when they first started. If many are using packaged systems and are satisfied, then you can probably do the same thing.

Handling Cash

There are several simple procedures that should be followed for handling cash. I'm including them not because they're new and exciting, but because they are too often ignored or neglected. These procedures are:

- Open a business checking account.
  - —Deposit cash receipts in it daily.
  - —Make all (except very small) payments by check. Never pay bills from cash receipts.
- Don't allow personal cash to get mixed up with business cash.
- Record all incoming cash, the amount, the source, and the date.
- Set up a petty cash account.
  - —Open and refill it with checks on the business account.
  - —Petty cash receipts, with proper amounts, should be filled out for each disbursement.
- Don't pay bills until an invoice is received. Then stamp the invoice paid and write the check number on the invoice. A file of paid invoices will avoid duplicate payments.

Use of Percentages

Percentages are an extremely useful tool when comparing financial data or other records (inventory stock outs, bad debts, etc.).

Percent change from one recordkeeping period to another provides insight into trends. For example, a 10% increase in returns from the first quarter to the second quarter might suggest that a quality control problem is developing.

Percentages of the whole can also be calculated from data within an accounting period. For example, returns can be calculated as a percentage of gross sales:

$$\text{Return percentage} = \frac{\substack{\text{dollar value of} \\ \text{returned goods}}}{\substack{\text{gross sales} \\ \text{for period}}} = \frac{\$2,000}{\$100,000} = 2\,\text{percent}$$

If returns remain as a constant percentage of sales in comparable accounting periods, there probably isn't any problem. Because if one sells more, one can expect a proportionate increase in returns.

Of course, the accounts analysis that utilizes balance sheets and income statement ratios is actually a percentage analysis. But, percentage analysis can be taken much further. Each business has unique characteristics and experiences unique phenomena that can be easily understood once appropriate percentages are calculated. I've found that customized percentages are very useful. In fact, often the more customized they are the more useful they are.

Budgeting

Everybody who has supervisory or management experience with any big company is familiar with budgeting. Big companies put a great deal of emphasis on budgeting, and rightly so.

But, many small businesses, especially when they are new, might ignore budgets. Frequently the reason given goes something like this, "How can I prepare a budget, when I don't have a track record to use for making estimates? Until I get some experience, I'm not going to be able to budget."

My answer to this is that if budgets aren't developed and used from the start, the experience one is accumulating could well be leading one right toward bankruptcy. Sure, initial budgets are difficult to prepare. Sales forecasts are less than accurate. It is hard to anticipate all expenses. But don't let these barriers stand in your way. Make best estimates. Make educated guesses. Remember, that an incomplete road map is better than none at all.

For many of us, experience in a big company has put a bad taste in our mouths for budgets and budgeting. "Sorry we can't give you a raise," says the big-company manager. "There is no money in the budget." Or the boss says, "Bill, that budget you prepared for next year has been kicked back. It's too high. You've got to trim it by 15%. Have it back to me tomorrow. Thanks." Just remember that as a big company employee, most of us were on the receiving end of the budget. It limited our salary or it represented an unpleasant task. But, as soon as you own your own small business, the roles are reversed. The many benefits of the budgeting process as a planning and control tool accrue to you, the owner.

Here again, I recommend that you utilize the advice of an accounting service or accounting professional to assist in setting up the appropriate budget. And be sure to include a cash budget. A cash flow forecast can prevent a disaster. And later, when excessive cash accumulates, this forecast will assist in guiding expansion or short-term investment.

Audits

As you probably know, big companies have their books audited yearly by certified public accountants. Small businesses generally do not require periodic audits. However, there are circumstances where audits are common. Banks or other lending institutions may require audited statements for loan approval purposes. And the purchaser of an ongoing small business may request an audit.

The reason audits are not common among small businesses is their high cost. A comprehensive audit, especially the first one, takes a good deal of time. (As I've mentioned, a CPA's time costs $20 to $70 an hour.) So an audit of the books of a modest size company might cost $3,000 to $5,000.

But audits do have a bright side. Often the thorough examinations uncover bookkeeping practices that, if changed, could lower income taxes. For example, delinquent receivables quite properly should be classified as bad debt.

Making Comparisons

Retailing operating ratios were discussed in Chapter 4. This type of ratio information is available (from the souces listed there) for many different types of businesses. Also many trade associations provided composite or coded financial information for their members.

Initially, this type of ratio information can be very helpful in preparing budgets. It may also be instructive to compare your business's results to those of other businesses of similar size and type. When doing this, however, keep in mind that differences in accounting procedures and practices may distort comparisons.

The most common comparison information available comes from major income statement items, such as cost of goods sold, rent, etc. If one of your ratios (i.e., percentages) is atypical, you may well have discovered an opportunity for corrective action and improvement.

Your Business Year

Most businesses, including most small businesses, utilize an annual accounting period (or year end) that corresponds to the calendar year; that is, their fiscal year ends on December 31 of each year.

But there is no requirement that you use that format. The Internal Revenue Service allows new taxpayers to adopt either a calendar year or a fiscal year (ending on the last day of some month other than December). It may be to your advantage to choose a noncalendar fiscal year. The most appropriate fiscal year end to adopt is when:

- Business activity is at a low point in the annual business cycle.
- Inventories are at their lowest.
- Accounts receivable are strong.

Adopting a noncalendar fiscal year has some other fringe benefits. Accountants have more time to do a thoughtful and careful job of closing the books and filing tax returns during nonpeak months. And inventory taking is easier because employees may be more available.

Electronic Data Processing

Electronic data processing equipment has now been reduced in price sufficiently to bring its services within the reach of many small businesses. Some banks and computer services offer payroll processing. Data terminals installed at a company's offices allow access to a large, time-shared computer that can perform a wide range of accounting functions. Minicomputers (for use in accounting, inventory control, process control, etc.) are widely available.

These services and this equipment are highly tempting. They not only promise to simplify operations and reduce costs, but they also are status symbols. But my advice to you is to avoid computerization until your business is well established and running smoothly. This will provide you time for making manually (and much more easily) those changes and adjustments that are always needed during startup or change-of-ownership transactions.

I'd be cautious about computerization even when a business is well-established. Computers are only as good as the people who operate them and the people who service them.

Finding Help

Betty Fuller decided to start a day-care center almost 10 years ago. Her timing couldn't have been more perfect. More wives were going back to work. The divorce rate was increasing.

Betty started with a preschool. A year later, demand prompted her to include a kindergarten. She was succeeding well beyond expectations, but felt swamped by rapid expansion and increased financial complexities. She said, "I'm a nurse and child-care expert, not a bookkeeper and financial expert."

Out of sheer frustration, Betty turned to a local financial services company that specializes in helping small companies with accounting, tax preparation, budget analysis, and financial planning. With the immediate pressures of recordkeeping and financial planning removed, Betty has been able to concentrate on her business and its growth. Now, 7 years later, she has 3 schools and a transportation company—all prospering!

It's quite common for a small business person to reach a point in the growth and maturity of his or her business where recordkeeping and financial planning become too much of a burden. If you plan to do your own recordkeeping initially, watch for this plateau. When it arrives, be flexible enough to consider a change.

You'll be amazed at the insights an accounting/financial adviser can bring to situations. One key business function in our inflationary society, is monitoring margins. They'll advise price increases when margins are no longer sufficient.

I started this treatment of accounting and recordkeeping by recommending outside professional assistance. And I'm going to end it that way. Don't try to set up and/or handle accounting and recordkeeping unless you have appropriate knowledge and experience.

REGULATIONS AND LICENSES.

If you decide to enter business, you're going to have to find out what licenses you'll need and what regulations affect you. Don't expect to get this information from any book. Although some books deal in great detail with regulations and licenses, they are not going to tell you what you need to know. That's because most regulations and licenses are local in nature.

The requirements for filing a fictitious-name statement, for example, are entirely different from locale to locale. The same is true for state unemployment insurance and workman's compensation laws and regulations.

Your lawyer, accountant, and county clerk will be helpful. But I'd also talk with established business owners in your community. They'll be able to tell you specifically what's required. They will also be able to share their real-world experience with you concerning licenses and regulations. We all know that the law is one thing and the way it's enforced can be, and often is, quite something else.

This brings me to the other message I want to get across concerning regulations and licenses. Let me tell you about Sam, the Tire Man. Sam Lorenzo owns five tire stores and a tire retreading plant in and around Carbondale, Illinois.

Following the Korean War, Sam went to work for Goodyear Tire in Akron, Ohio, as an order-entry clerk. Next he was a territory salesman and industrial tire sales manager in Peoria, Illinois. Then he was transferred back to headquarters.

When he found out the Carbondale dealership was available, he decided to strike off on his own. That was in 1955. And do you know what? From that very first year, right up until now, Sam has been actively involved in efforts to improve the regulatory climate for small business the Illinois and throughout the nation.

Over the years, Sam has mounted efforts to lobby against government regulation in the tire business. One current effort involves federal new-tire registration. This regulation mandates that the dealer register the sale of each new tire. Sam and his followers emphasize that this registration has become oppressively costly and does little or no good, anyway. In 1975, it cost about 40 cents for a tire dealer to register a purchase. By 1980, the cost had risen to over $2.

The tire dealer has no choice but to tack this cost onto the price of a tire. A survey of new-tire purchasers found that 8 out of 10 of them would prefer a simpler do-it-yourself system, like the warrantee cards filled out for major appliance purchases.

The irony of this particular government regulation is that despite its oppressive cost, it isn't being administered adequately. There are over 200,000 tire dealers across the country, but the government has only 10 people to administer the program! They're probably buried in Washington under tons of registration forms.

Another uphill battle Sam has been fighting focuses on the plight of the small business person in Illinois. He feels that future expansion of small business in Illinois depends to a great extent on how the state government handles unemployment insurance and workman's compensation regulations.

Business costs in these areas have been skyrocketing lately and are much higher than in neighboring states. For example, during the last 4 years, Lorenzo's state-mandated workman's compensation insurance has gone up by a factor of 4½ (for the same number of employees)! And incredibly, unemployment insurance costs have gone up even more. For example, 4 years ago Sam's costs were about .5 percent of his payroll. Now they are over 4 percent of payroll expenses. Unfortunately, Sam's expense is not unique. These rapid cost increases have hit employers throughout the state.

Sam Lorenzo has been lobbying hard and long for his causes. He is chairman of the Small Business Council of the Illinois State Chamber of Commerce, as well as president of his local chamber of commerce. Although he hasn't won any big battles, he says he will continue to fight. "Recently, for the first time, I think people are really listening," says Sam, with a determined look in his eye.

All of us who are self-employed should admire Sam Lorenzo for what he is doing. And even more importantly, we should all follow his example. It's one thing to find out about licenses and regulations so we can all learn to live with them. But that's not enough. More of us have to get involved. We have to fight oppressive and unnecessary regulations. They are bad for small business people and bad for consumers.

TAXES.

Every dollar you don't have to pay in taxes is a dollar you get to reinvest in your business or keep for yourself. This is not to suggest that you should cheat on business taxes. But, most people have learned that paying only what is required is a virtue for personal taxes. Well, the same is true for business taxes.

Paying only what is required on business taxes, unfortunately, is even more complicated and perplexing than it is on personal taxes. That's probably why experts on preparing business tax returns were around and thriving long before H & R Block prepared their first personal tax return. The message in all this should be clear. To pay only what is required (no more and no less) demands the touch of an expert. Yet too many fledgling small business persons filed "do-it-yourself" tax returns. This is foolish, plain and simple.

Hiring an expert doesn't abrogate your responsibility as a business owner in the eyes of federal and state taxing bodies. So you've got to be aware of basic guidelines and principles. The following sections describe some of the most salient points, according to experts.

Complete and Accurate Records

I know that to bring this topic up again is like beating a dead horse, but the whole tax situation is a beautiful opportunity to reemphasize this essential point for small business success. There is no way a business income tax return will stand up to audit without substantiating records. And there is no way even the owner can be sure he or she is paying the proper amount of taxes without proper records.

Plan to keep your records for several years. The IRS says, "records *must* be retained as long as their contents may become material in the administration of any Internal Revenue law." Who knows how long that is? The IRS has a publication *Guide to Records Retention Requirements* if you're interested. My personal policy has always been to keep everything forever. If space is a problem, use microfilm. Hard copies can then be made upon request.

Initial Elections and Choices

Certain options are available to a new business which can have a profound impact on tax obligations. The tax angle should be carefully considered at each decision point. Here are some of the more critical elections and choices:

- Accounting method—most common are cash receipts and disbursements, and accrual. There are pros and cons for each. The nature of the business may negate the cash option.
- Accounting period (see previous discussion in this chapter).
- Amortization of corporation organizational expenses.
- Direct change-off of bad debt, or reserve method.
- Treatment of research and experimental expenditures.
- Reporting income on installment method.
- Amortization of circulation expenditures.
- Reporting income from long-time construction contracts on a percentage of completion contracts method.
- Accelerated depreciation methods.
- Inventory pricing methods.

- Pension and profit sharing plans.
- Amortization of trademarks and trade names.
- Amortization of bond premiums.

Just scanning the above list reinforces my position that tax matters are not for amateurs. One other note: Some of these elections are irreversible. Others, like the choice of accounting period, can be changed at a future date.

Lease vs Buy

The leasing of business equipment (including vehicles) has become more and more popular, partly because of tax advantages. Lease payments are deductible, whereas the cost of purchasing an asset is depreciated. Comparison of these two approaches often shows an advantage to leasing.

But other considerations, besides taxes, must also be evaluated. Is capital available for purchase? If not, and you prefer not to increase debt, then leasing may be the answer. Resale value is another factor. If the item in question has little resale value or if it will be used in such a way as to detract from its value (e.g., excessive wear), than a lease arrangement might be preferred.

Calling Your Shots

The timing of everyday business decisions can affect your income tax liability. For example, if you are on a cash accounting system and a calendar fiscal year, paying invoices in January of the upcoming year instead of December of the current year will lower your gross income for the current year.

Another example is discretionary expenses. If you are having a very good year, it might be wise to spend a little extra on repairs, maintenance, redecorating, etc. The reverse is also true. If delaying such expenses to next year will give you a tax advantage, then do so. It's legal.

There are literally dozens of these opportunities. Some are so clever and so specialized that it takes CPAs to recognize and recommend them. And don't think these techniques are limited to small business. Big corporations are experts at shifting income and expenses from one accounting period to the next. The crux of a decision to sell off a whole division this year might hinge on tax considerations.

Sole Proprietorships

Sole proprietors (and, in many respects, partners) have a somewhat special income tax situation. A sole proprietor of a business does not file a business income tax return. Rather, he or she includes business income on the personal income tax return.

Therefore, one must take care to separate business expenses from personal expenses (which are not deductible). Operating the business out of one's home and using a car for both business and personal reasons are just two of the complicating factors.

Basically, the overall guideline is that you can deduct as business expenses all ordinary and necessary expenses you incur to earn your income.

Also, sole proprietors will likely be liable for self-employment tax. This tax is in place of the social security tax one pays as an employee. But it is higher (because the employer is no longer kicking in his share). Sole proprietors usually are required to file a declaration of estimated tax and to make estimated tax payments.

Leaseholder Improvements

Leaseholder improvements are usually considered as capital expenditures and not as deductible current expenses.

The business owner's (i.e., the leaseholder's) costs of making permanent improvements on property leased for business use are only recoverable through deductions each year in one of two ways: over the remaining life of the lease, or over the estimated life of the improvement, whichever is shorter. Improvement costs recovered over the life of the lease must be amortized, while improvement costs recovered over the life of the improvement can be depreciated. Whether a lease has a renewal clause may also be a factor in determining the recovery period.

IRS regulations and explanations on this and any other deduction go on almost ad nauseam. I won't mimic the errant ways of the government here. Just remember, if you make permanent improvements to leased property, you've probably got some form of deduction coming. Your accountant can adivse you.

Depreciation

A good many people who are interested in starting their own business don't quite know what depreciation is, or how to calculate it. If you're in this group, don't feel bad. Depreciation is a nebulous concept. And the ins and outs of determining depreciation to the business owner's best advantage are beyond the capability of most nonexperts.

In this section I just want to present the fundamentals of depreciation. With these you'll be able to ask your accountant the right questions, and then he or she can handle the specifics.

By the way, if you are among the few who are comfortable with the basics of depreciation, I'm sorry for boring you with this. But I don't feel that I have any choice. Depreciation is a key business concept. It is important for everybody to know what it is all about.

Suppose you own a business and have a business telephone. The monthly cost of that telephone is a business *expense*, which means that you can deduct it from your yearly gross income (along with all your other business expenses) to determine your taxable net income. Other business expenses include rent, office supplies, insurance, etc.

Now just suppose you buy some new office furniture for your business. Surely, you assume, this also is a business expense. But the accountants and the IRS don't feel that it is proper to deduct the entire cost of a capital investment (furniture, a machine, an automobile) during the year in which it is purchased. Rather, some portion of the cost of the investment is deducted from gross income each year, over the item's useful life. So depreciation is an expense deduction that lets you recover (or deduct) your capital investment (in buildings, machinery, and other items used in your business) over the useful life of the capital investment. Simple, isn't it?

There are several things you should know about determining depreciation for a particular capital expense. First, depreciation can be calculated in several different ways: the straight-line method, declining balance, sum-of-the-years digits, and others. Which method you use can have a sizable impact on your income tax obligation. Understanding the tax laws concerning depreciation and applying these laws properly in a particular situation are best left to the experts in the field.

Finally, there is such a thing as additional first-year depreciation. The IRS says, "You may elect to deduct 20% of the cost of qualified property as additional first year depreciation in addition to your regular depreciation." Your accountant will be able to explain this option to you.

Part-Time Businesses

There is a special tax problem associated with part-time or sideline businesses that operate in the red. The problem is in differentiating the legitimate businesses (that are struggling to make a profit but are falling short) from businesses that are actually hobbies in disguise. If hobbyists can get away with camouflaging their activities as business, all the expenses associated with the hobby can be deducted from their primary income (which is probably a wage or salary).

Dog breeders are famous for this tactic. Some are operating real businesses, but I think that most are just dog fanciers who can't resist the temptation to deduct the cost of dog food and the expenses associated with dog shows.

If you start a part-time business and it initially operates in the red, be prepared to demonstrate your profit-making expectations. Relevant information includes the amount of time you spend, the reason for your loss, and the lack of a dominant element of recreation or pleasure. Also, if you show a profit in 2 or more years during a 5-year period, the IRS will accept your for-profit intentions.

Federal Employee Taxes

Now we get to the portion of the federal bureaucracy that drives many small business persons crazy. Again I quote from the IRS: "As an employer, you will be responsible for withholding and paying certain taxes in connection with the salaries, wages, tips, and other compensation paid to your employees . . . you as an employer are liable for payments to the government of the various taxes withheld from your employees' compensation and you are subject to penalties for nonpayment."

We've all been on the receiving end of this message. It's the big chunk taken out of every paycheck for social security (Federal Insurance Contributions Act), income tax, and so on. If you decide to become an employer, you've got to do the taking out and the paying to the government. (And let's not forget that the same goes for state taxes, such as sales taxes.)

All this collecting and paying amounts to additional time and additional paper work. So be prepared for it. It's part of the hassle that goes with the joys of owning and running one's own business.

The rules, regulations, and procedures covering all this, if collected in one stack, could make a major metropolitan telephone book look pint-size by comparison.

Happily, the accountants and their accounting procedures, systems, and expertise come to the rescue again. Rely on your accountant.

By the way, there is a way to avoid having employees in some circumstances. Instead of hiring people, you can contract with them to provide a service to you. If it's applicable to your situation, it will greatly simplify and minimize your employer tax obligations.

IRA and Keogh Plans

There is no excuse for not having an individual retirement savings program (IRA) or a Keogh Plan if you are self-employed. As a matter of fact, you don't even have to be self-employed to qualify for an IRA—as long as your employer doesn't have a plan.

Both the IRA and the Keogh allow a person to deduct a percentage of their annual income from federal income taxes. These are set aside to provide retirement benefits. And both the amount set aside yearly and the earnings realized from them each year are free of immediate tax. Taxes are not due until these funds are taken out of the IRA or Keogh Plan. Also under certain circumstances, withdrawals are given special beneficial tax treatments.

An IRA or a Keogh Plan is a great tax shelter. Talk to your accountant about establishing the plan that is most beneficial to you.

Small Business as a Marvelous Tax Dodge

Some people have the notion that small businesses, especially unincorporated ones, are marvelous tax dodges. It's quite popular for business brokers, for example, to suggest to a novice potential purchaser that a particular business is a fantastic tax haven. The inference being that one can deduct items such as a car or a sailboat or a mountain retreat from the income of the business.

Let's get it straight. The idea of a small business being a great tax dodge, as promoted by hucksters and believed only by the naïve, is tremendously overstated.

I went to a small business opportunity exhibition last year where one exhibitor continually alluded to the tax advantage of being self-employed. He was selling franchises for a line of prepackaged health food products. But when I cornered him and pinned him down, he admitted that the only tax benefits he was able to realize were modest deductions for an at-home office and business-related transportation expenses. Big deal! If he was lucky, he was deducting perhaps a thousand dollars, which might have saved him at most $250 a year in income taxes.

I'd suggest that you get your hands on the IRS publication *Tax Guide for Small Businesses* (No. 334). It will set you straight on legitimate business deductions. It's also a good basic primer on everything from business structures to accounting principles. Another publication that I highly recommend is *Small-Time Operator* (Bell Springs Publishing) by Bernard Kamoroff. He is a CPA with the unusual knack of putting apparently complicated accounting and tax matters into easily understood language.

FOURTEEN

Employees—getting the most out of them.

"Employees are a pain in the neck," so says Bill Murray, a man who owns a ServiceMaster residential cleaning service. Bill explains, "They're never satisfied with the pay. They want more and more time off. They all want to be crew chiefs. They're sick too often. They're late too often. They all need training, but they have no loyalty. It seems that some just work long enough to go onto unemployment."

Bill Murray is much more vocal about his employee problems then most, but his stance on the difficulties of being an employer is not atypical. Bill sounds as though he's about ready to give it all up because of his people problems. But that's not the case at all. He's just venting steam. Actually he has learned over time how to accept and cope effectively with the human factor in his business.

You will have to do the same thing. Depending on the type of business you enter, your problems with employees could be much less difficult than Bill's, or they could be even more trying. In any case, here is some advice and information that will be helpful.

INVEST IN PEOPLE.

"The guys who are making it are the guys who are investing in their employees." It may be hard to believe, but this quote is from the same Bill Murray who says, "Employees are a pain in the neck." And you know what? He's sincere when he says "invest in people," for that's exactly what he does. Not because he's a good guy, but because he's practical and pragmatic. He knows it takes good people to make his business go. As Bill says, "Nobody has invented a machine yet that will clean carpets and furniture by itself." Bill knows that his employees are going to do him wrong once in a while, but he accepts it and invests in them despite it, for his own good and for his employees' good.

A GOOD MAN (OR WOMAN) IS HARD TO FIND.

Remember the old popular song "A Good Man Is Hard To Find"? Most women would agree, even today, that this romantic observation is true. And most small business owners would concur that good people are hard to find.

The problem is that there is always a shortage of capable people, and small businesses must compete for these people with the Fords and the K-Marts and Prudentials of the world.

Big corporations are tough competition. They usually can offer higher wages and, almost always a better benefits package. Plus, they offer an identity that employees can relate to: "Oh, I work for IBM" or "I'm in purchasing at Sears."

When the demand for people heats up, big corporations have the money and the clout to attract job candidates. Right now "body hunting" is going on at a feverish pace in an area of California called Silicon Valley. The U.S. semiconductor industry is concentrated in this area and the market for products of this type has been expanding so rapidly that all the producers are shorthanded. One company spokesman says, "Others are worse off than we are. Our company *only* has 250 openings." Not surprisingly, the semiconductor producers are offering all kinds of inducements—including 2-month paid sabbaticals after 5 years of service, hiring-on bonuses of $1,000, $2,000, or even $3,000, cash rewards to current employees who bring in a hirable candidate, and so on.

I wouldn't like to be the owner of a small, fledgling business in

Silicon Valley (i.e., Santa Clara County) right now. Especially if it is trying to hire people with the same job skills as the semiconductor industry is seeking.

But all is not gloom. Seasoned small business people have found ways to attract good people to their organizations and to keep most of them there. The key is to emphasize the unique advantages of working for and being a part of a smaller company. These include:

- A warm, personal working atmosphere
- No possiblity that a new employee will get lost in the crowd
- Greater advancement opportunities (because of the greater expansion potential of smaller businesses)
- More responsibility and challenge
- Greater sense of accomplishment
- Opportunity for exposure to many facets of business, rather than being pidgeon-holed

All of these are true advantages of working for a smaller company. Emphasize them in your recruiting efforts and in your regular conversation with employees. Job satisfaction is important to people. In fact, it's becoming more important than money in a lot of instances. Small businesses offer job satisfaction. That's why so many people long to be their own boss. For those who can't be their own boss, you can offer an attractive alternative—being part of a small business.

BEGIN WITH BASICS.

Assembling an efficient and productive group of employees begins with attention to basic human resource principles. The first of these is a plan for both immediate and longer-term pesonnel needs. How many full-time people are required? How many part-time? What job is each to perform (clerk, delivery truck driver, warehouse order picker, etc.)? Much of the input for this effort will come from your initial business planning. After all, to project a first-year income statement, you must have estimated a first-year cost for payroll expense. Now the specific jobs that add up to this total estimate must be defined. Hopefully, some thought has already gone into this, since the best way to estimate payroll expense is to count heads or workerhours at each wage level and then multiply.

Next, a job description should be prepared for each specific position. Its purpose is to document and describe the major or primary responsibilities associated with a job. It should not be exhaustive in detail, but rather, capture the essence of the task in precise and simple terms.

Job specifications are also needed. These define the qualifications required for successful performance of the job. Particulars include experience, education, skills, etc.

If your business requires a formal organization structure, now is the time to lay it out. Employees are more comfortable when they know who their immediate boss is, and what the chain of command is.

Now you're ready to organize your recruiting plans and programs. For these, your goal should be to attract enough applicants for each position so that you have a reasonable choice, rather than being forced to select the best of a small group of poor candidates. Depending on your specific business situation, you may be staffing an entire new organization (for example, if you purchase a new fast-food franchise) or only filling one position (if you buy a one-person business but need a part-time assistant to extend business hours). In any case, plan ahead and give it your best effort.

USING TEMPORARY HELP.

Temporary help agencies are available for both office and industrial work. Although the hourly rates are higher than a business would pay for a permanent employee, certain advantages may offset that. For one thing, temporary means just that—temporary. You pay only for exactly the hours you need: an extra person for that busy time on sale days, for emergency snow removal, or whatever. This could save you from overtaxing your permanent employees or from losing sales. Temporary help also saves you a good deal of paper work and withholding tax complications. Training may also be eliminated if the agency can supply a person with the proper experience.

A friend of mine owns an extremely successful temporary industrial help agency. He tells me that most of his business comes from regular, repeat customers. This surprised me. You would think that any business that has a continuing need for help would hire a full-time or part-time employee. But they don't always do that.

The best business organization is the one that is lean. Maintain your flexibility and your profits by using temporary help to your advantage.

PERSONNEL RECORD SYSTEMS.

Yes, I'm sorry to say it, but here comes more paper work. This is another one of the topics that authors typically avoid, because they feel that it will discourage potential book buyers. No one wants to be told, or reminded, that he or she is going to have to keep records on all the business's employees. But that's the reality of the situation. I promised when I started this book that I was going to tell it like it is. I've been doing just that up until now, so why stop?

Every company I've ever worked for (both big and small) has had a file on me and every other employee. I'm sure your employers have had them, too. And your business, if you decide to start or purchase a business, will have to keep a file on every employee. It's just part of the game, like it or not.

My suggestion, with this and other apparent detractions from the joy of owning one's own business, is to emphasize the positive. If you've got to have employee records, use them to your advantage. Make your records work for you, not against you.

Personnel records are the only tangible chronology of the owner's investment in his or her employees. An accurate, complete, and responsive system will contribute to employee morale, payroll monitoring and control, employee motivation, and a host of other aspects of business health.

I once worked for a company where just the opposite was true.

Their personnel record system stank—to put it bluntly. The company didn't know how many vacation days some employees had taken. Semi-annual performance and salary reviews were delayed or entirely missed because the tickler system was awkward and cumbersome. I have no doubt that all this confusion contributed to high employee turnover and poor employee performance.

One pitfall that many new small business owners fall into is to begin with an incomplete or inadequate system. "What the heck," the owner of a travel agency told me, "when I started it was just me and two part-timers. I didn't think I needed any formal records. I kept it all in my head. But after I added a few more people and after some time had passed, I realized I couldn't remember if all; I forgot Evelyn's first anniversary. I even forgot to increase one person's salary after I promised her I would. And I had no idea about tardiness and days absent. What I did have was a mess."

So, even if you start small, start right. Low-cost, prepackaged personnel record systems are available. You may never have an official personnel department, but you will have a personnel function—even with only one or two employees. Simple personnel record systems will allow you to keep track of employee hiring, payroll, promotions, transfers, layoffs, etc. Accurate documentation of your decisions as an employer—from hiring through employee separations—can also aid you in complying with the various state and federal nondiscrimination and equal employment opportunity laws and regulations.

USE INCENTIVE COMPENSATION WHENEVER POSSIBLE.

I am a strong believer in using compensations to motivate people. This technique is especially critical in a small, new business that needs to get the most out of each employee.

Historically, the most common form of incentive compensation was the piece-rate system used in manufacturing or production situations. This approach is fine, but it is only one application of the "carrot" compensation system.

I know of a large management consulting organization that has promoted and implemented incentive compensation systems in almost all functional business areas (clerical, engineering, staff positions, maintenance, etc.) and in many types of industries.

Sales, of course, is a natural functional area for incentive compensation. Here the incentive compensation plan options include a total-incentive approach or a base-salary-plus-incentive. The base-salary-plus-incentive is most popular. But, for a new company or for the purpose of launching a new product, it is quite common to adopt an agency or commission approach to avoid the fixed cost of a salaried sales force, to spread the risk between the company and the sales organization, and to maximize the sales force's incentive to develop the market.

In sales department salary plus-incentive systems, a common practice is to have about 75 percent of the total compensation fixed with the remainder somehow tied to output. This incentive portion can take several forms. The most widely known is the commission arrangment, in which a commission is usually paid on total sales or sales over a given quota.

Another form of incentive is the bonus. Bonuses are usually paid quarterly or yearly and are based on sales volume or other measures (such as sales potential in a territory, historic sales performance, etc.).

A combination of commission and sales bonuses can also be used in conjunction with a fixed salary. The options are many and should be matched to the particular business situation.

I presented a brief overview of sales department incentive compensation systems because I want to emphasis that incentive compensation can easily and fruitfully be applied to almost all jobs within a small business.

I'd suggest a fixed salary plus bonus and/or commission. A marvelous advantage of a commission incentive is that it is payable weekly or monthly. Frequent payments result in a closer relationship between compensation and performance. And since workers in a small business naturally feel that what they do *really* does have an

impact, the incentive pay reinforces and stimulates this sense of satisfaction.

Working out an equitable and meaningful fixed salary plus incentive system may take some experimentation and may not always go
smoothly. But at least consider it. If nothing else, institute an
employee suggestion system with cash savings tied directly to the
savings realized by the business. You'd be amazed at how creative
and ingenious people are when they know that their ego and their
pocket books will be rewarded.

EMPLOYEE MOTIVATION.

"Don't expect your employees to work as hard as you do," so
speaks a successful small business owner. Then he cautions, "And if
by some quirk an employee does want to work as hard as you do,
don't let him. Because if you do, either he will get fed up and quit, or
his wife will get fed up and then he will quit."

It sounds as if this business owner is saying that there is no way to
win. And in some respects, he is probably right. Only a small business
owner has the motivation of a small business owner. And only his or
her spouse could possibly understand that motivation.

In reality, I don't think employers have to worry too much about
the overmotivated worker. Rather, it's the vast majority of workers
performing at 80 percent or 70 percent or even 60 percent of capacity who cause headaches.

Compensation as a motivation has been discussed already. But
there are other potent motivational tools. A landmark book on the
subject of employee motivation in business was written by the late
Douglas McGregor, of the Massachusetts Institute of Technology, in
1960. In his book, *The Human Side of Enterprise*, McGregor advanced the proposition that the way a boss relates to employees is a
key ingredient for motivation.[1]

McGregor observed that some managers inspired workers, gain-

[1]Douglas McGregor, *The Human Side of Enterprise,* McGraw-Hill, 1960.

ing their support and wholehearted effort, while other managers alienated their people and constantly bickered with them. After much study, McGregor concluded that a manager's attitude toward his or her subordinates was the prime distinction.

Thus was born the famous "Theory X" and "Theory Y." "Theory X" managers, the inspirational motivators, felt that people enjoy work and will work toward the objectives of their organization if they receive recognizable rewards for doing so. Theory X also suggests that monitory rewards are insufficient; that recognition, a feeling of accomplishment, etc., are also important.

"Theory Y" managers' attitude toward their people results from their belief that people dislike work and will avoid it if possible. Therefore, this theory maintains that people must be coerced to work, and must be closely monitored.

The lesson here, I think, is clear. If one wants good results from employees, delegate responsibilities and authority. Allow them the freedom to meet their responsibilities. And reward them, both monetarily and emotionally, when they come through. Nurture a positive attitude—one that gives your employees the opportunity to produce.

EMPLOYEE BENEFITS.

Employee benefits are a fact of life. You and I expect them as an employee, so as a prospective employer, expect to offer them in your business.

Employee benefits are part—an important, expensive part—of employee compensation. They can account for up to 20 to 25 percent of a company's compensation costs.

Employee benefits can be broadly categorized as:

- *Budgeting programs.* These provide payment for expenses the employee usually could pay for from current income or savings. They typically require frequent but small payments. These programs include:

   —Dental insurance plan
   —Short-term disability plan
   —Maternity plan

• *Catastrophic insurance programs.* These are intended to provide
  economic protection for the small number of employees whose
  income is ended permanently. These programs include:

   —Life insurance
   —Long-term disability insurance

• *Retirement programs.* These are distinguished by the accumula-
  tion of large sums of money over an employee's career. At retirement an employee may have earned pension rights with a capital
  value equal to several times annual preretirement earnings. These
  programs include:

   —Pension plans
   —Deferred profit sharing plans

Some plans fit into more than one category. A medical insurance
plan, for example, will cover both a 3-day hospital stay (which most
employees could afford) and major surgery (which would bankrupt
most families).

Small businesses generally provide fewer benefits than big corporations. Few small businesses that I know of offer dental insurance or
retirement programs, for example. Your best bet, however, is to find
out what the practices are in your particular job market. Established
small business owners will be able to tell you.

THE SMALL BUSINESS TEAM.

Working with other people to accomplish a common goal is one of
life's most satisfying experiences. Small businesses are a special opportunity for a group of people to work together, to make things
happen, to build, and to have fun doing it.

Some of the most successful small businesses are those where
team work makes it happen.

FIFTEEN

Selling is success.

I've given a great deal of thought to how I should present the material in this last chapter. I've tried to come up with some attention-getting way of driving my message home. I've considered and discarded many ideas, including putting only one word on the first page of the chapter. That word would be S-E-L-L.

I want to shout this message as loudly as I can: In any small business, selling is success. Making it in a small business is both as simple and as extremely difficult as that.

A TRUE STORY.

Two and a half years ago, Bill Montgomery was vice-president and plant manager of a factory in Denver, making $28,000 a year. Suddenly, a transfer of manufacturing facilities to Minneapolis eliminated his job. Montgomery's company offered him the position of assistant plant manager in Minneapolis at the same salary.

But Bill and his family loved living in the foothills of the Rockies. They had just finished building a new home. Bill was planning to buy a used Jeep.

Being *assistant* plant manager and losing his vice-president title didn't sit well wth him, either. Especially since the Minneapolis plant manager was 20 years away from retirement age. Moving to Minneapolis, to Bill, seemed a step in the wrong direction for his company. When he joined the company 3 years earlier, he was told that the Denver plant would soon be enlarged and a new plant built on the west coast. Instead, came this retrenchment back to Minneapolis.

Bill and his wife, Judy, didn't know what to do. Moving to Minneapolis seemed all wrong, but quitting meant finding another job, if one were to be found. Ever since Judy and Bill met, Bill had talked about opening a restaurant someday—a pizza restaurant. Judy used to kid him by asking, "Why would a guy with a name like Montgomery want to start a pizza parlor?" "Because I like pizza, that's why!" Bill would jokingly shout back. "And I've got a terrific recipe."

But the time for joking about pizza seemed to have passed. "Judy and I had some money in the bank and we had a few stocks. Why not take the plunge? The opportunity might never come again." That's how Bill described the rationale that went into the decision to quit his job when the Denver plant closed.

Montgomery was in business 6 months later. He bought a small take-out pizza and sandwich business for $14,000. His plan was to expand it into a sit-down restaurant after he and Judy settled into the routine. At first Bill limited his efforts to delivering his pizza, ribs, sandwiches, and homemade onion soup to residents in a nice suburb of Denver. "There were times when I would take the order, cook it, and deliver it—all myself," recalls Montgomery.

The business was doing just about what the previous owner had been doing, which—unfortunately for Judy and Bill—wasn't very much. Average gross was about $100 to $120 a night. But this didn't discourage Bill, because he felt that sales would expand greatly when he had his sit-down facility with red checkered tablecloths, antiques, etc.

So Bill expanded. The old take-out portion became the kitchen and a large dining room was added by taking over the next storefront. "I thought it would cost about $10,000 to remodel the place and fix it up," Montgomery said, "but I had to knock a hole in the wall to connect it to my kitchen next door, the whole place had to be rewired and I wound up spending $28,000."

Through necessity, during the remodeling process Montgomery became a carpenter, a painter, and an electrician's assistant. Judy refinished 35 old-fashioned drugstore chairs and some pews purchased from a bankrupt church. The expansion was paid for with a loan from Judy's parents.

Keeping the carry-out business going and adding the dining room at the same time hurt Judy and Bill's personal life. "We began to lose most of our friends because we were always working and could never take the time to get together with them," Judy explained. "But we had made a commitment and we were determined to succeed. We had sunk everything into this business—even the future of our two children."

The new dining room opened on the first anniversary of the day Bill sold his first pizza. Not long after that, the Montgomerys began to wonder what was going on.

"We were really proud of our new dining room. It was comfortable, uniquely decorated, clean, on a busy street and in a good neighborhood. Everything the restaurant experts say you need to succeed," Bill recalls. "But it just sat there. It just didn't take off like we though it would. It was taking in maybe $40 to $60 a night on average. We were losing money and were so discouraged. I decided we were having trouble because nobody knew about our dining room. So I put ads in the local paper, and I shelled out $1,200 for a new electric sign to hang in the front. Guess what? No difference. Still $40 to $60 a night, maybe $60 to $70 on weekends."

WHAT'S WRONG?

Bill and Judy's pizza restaurant was in danger of collapsing. Bill's dream of owning a prosperous pizza restaurant was fast becoming a horrible nightmare.

What was going wrong? Well, the simple, superficial answer was that pizza wasn't selling for the Montgomerys. But why wasn't it? The people who did come in said they enjoyed it. And some had even come back again.

Let's take a look at the figures. Bill was averaging $50 a night in the dining room. He was open 6 nights for, say, 50 weeks a year. The take-out business was still averaging $110 per night. So here is Bill's gross annualized income (that is, his sales):

	Daily average		Days/week		Week/years		Yearly total
Dining room	$ 50	×	6	×	50	=	$15,000
Take out	110	×	6	×	50	=	33,000
							$48,000

This $48,000 doesn't look too bad until you look at the expense side of the statment:

Category	Annualized cost
Food and supplies	$18,000
Payroll	17,000
Rent	2,400
Other (laundry, uniforms, garbage, exterminating, utilities, legal works, accounting, repairs, insurance, etc.)	6,000
Total	$43,400

So we see that the Montgomerys were just barely in the black. And the $17,000 payroll expense didn't include any takehome pay for Judy or Bill. It all went for one part-time cook, two waitresses, a dishwasher, and several part-time delivery people. So, Bill's takehome was only about $4,600 a year ($48,000 − $43,400). A long shot from his old salary of $28,000 and not anywhere near enough to support a family of four.

By the way, the interest (usually due the lender) on the money Bill put into the business ($14,000 plus $28,000) wasn't included in Bill's expenses. If he had included this, at a 10 percent rate, he would be only a few hundred dollars away from red ink. Bill gets a break here because all the invested capital is family money. But, if the $42,000 were invested elsewhere, it could earn from 5 to 10 percent, or more, so it should really be recognized as a cost—or as a return on invested capital that the business should produce above and beyond the proprietor's salary.

A Happy Ending

After 6 months of excruciatingly slow dining room business, at Judy's insistence and against Bill's original plans, the Montgomerys bought a liquor license and began selling beer and wine. "I didn't want to sell alcohol because I can't stand drunks," explained Bill. "But after I began, I found out that people don't come to a pizza joint to get drunk. They come to eat, and maybe parents or a couple have beer or wine. And it hasn't destroyed the family-type atmosphere I was striving for."

The availability of wine and beer did raise dining room business tremendously. Instead of averaging $50 a night in the dining room, after 6 months with a liquor license, the Montgomerys were grossing about $150 on week nights and almost twice that on Fridays and Saturdays.

Annualized gross sales for the dining room and take-out now total about $95,000 a year and are still climbing. After all expenses, Bill now can take home a salary about equal to his $28,000 as a plant manager.

Bill is happy. He put it this way: "My hours are long and hard, but if I had to do over again, I would do the same thing. I like working for myself, being self-made, so to speak. I don't like being told that the company is consolidating and eliminating my job. The only person who can eliminate my job now is me. See this restaurant? It's mine. It's a hassle, but I really love it. Don't ask me why, but I just love it."

THE MESSAGE.

Just opening a store or restaurant, or manufacturing a product does not make a going business.

The location, products, services, an accountant's help, incorporation, and all the other activities which apparently make a business go—in reality are subservient to one essential business ingredient: selling. You can have a great location but if you're not selling, forget it. You can have a terrifically clever new product made from the best materials, but if it's not selling, you're dead. You can have the best accounting and cost control system, but if you don't have the sales volume, it's meaningless.

The Montgomerys found this out. Their delicious pizzas, their good location, and their attractive decor weren't enough. What they needed, of all things, was a liquor license. The license wasn't an end in itself, only a means of *giving the customers what they wanted.*

This is the message: Give the customers what they want (whether it be a Pet Rock, pizzas with alcohol available, or whatever) and you will sell and you will succeed.

Henry Ford, the man who revolutionized the production of the automobile, put it this way: "The man who will use his skill and constructive imagination to see how much he can give for a dollar, instead of how little he can give for a dollar, is bound to succeed."

The subservience to selling of all other business activities can also be viewed in terms of a business owner's specific knowledge and experience. Some knowledge of all areas of business management (e.g., finance, accounting, manufacturing, distribution, personnel administration, etc.) is helpful to a small business person, but one can easily succeed on sales ability alone. Financial advice can be purchased. Accountants can be hired, manufacturing expertise can be found, distribution consultants are available, personnel managers can be brought on board. All these skills can be bought, but the one essential ingredient—selling—cannot be bought. Sure, you can hire salespeople and marketing skills, but if the basic premise of the business doesn't deliver what the customer wants, the sales effort will not succeed, no more than the best of Hollywood's hype and promotion can save a movie that's bombing.

Now, I'm not saying that if you're an accountant or a production foreman or a personnel manager, you can't succeed in a business of your own. What I'm saying is that skill in these areas is good, but probably not sufficient. Some sales skills and a product or service that gives customers what they want, will be needed.

An entrepreneur can buy accounting help, legal advice, management skills, production knowhow, but one thing he can't afford to buy is customers.

THE BOTTOM LINE.

A look at sales volume and profit numbers can tell us some important things that relate directly to selling as the key ingredient of business success.

I want to emphasize that selling, as I'm using it, means selling in sufficient volume to support the business owner in the life-style he or she desires. It's no doubt true that any business venture, no matter how poorly conceived and managed, will sell something to someone. I could probably place an ad in *Field and Stream*'s mail-order section offering a small box of paper clips for $1.98 plus $1.00 postage and handling and get an order or two. I'd be selling, but not succeeding.

Salary and Profit

This brings us to the first issue in this section on bottom-line topics: It's the question of owner's salary and net business profit. This is quite often an area of confusion because if is not clear in many cases if owner's salary has been deducted from net profit, or whether, on the other hand, net profit includes owner's salary. For example, a business that nets $5,000 after deduction of a $30,000 salary for the owner (assuming he or she is working in the business) is doing quite well. But a business that is netting $5,000 including owner's salary is paying the owner a paltry wage.

Actually, a business should produce a fair return on invested capital, after the deduction of a reasonable salary for the owner who works in the business and for any time put in by the owner's family. And the after-salary return should be at least equal to the earning power of outside investments (like savings accounts, corporate bonds, common stocks, or real estate).

Let's look at an example: A potential business owner expects a return of 10 percent on the capital he or she wants to invest in a business and feels that the effort required to run the business is worth

$30,000 per year in salary. Thus, a new business requiring $100,000 in capital (or a purchasable business costing $100,000) should return a total pretax profit of $40,000 (that's $10,000 return on investment and $30,000 in owner's salary).

Profits, Sales, and Customers Needed Per Day

Now that we recognize that the profit we expect from a business includes owner's salary plus return on investment, we can look at what this translates to in terms of required sales activity per day to produce this profit.

Let's stick with the $40,000 total pretax profit (as in the example above). To generate a $40,000 profit per year in 6 days a week means a profit per day of $40,000 ÷ (52 weeks × 6 days a week) = $128 profit per day.

Assume this business has a pretax net profit (after deducting owner's salary) of 5 percent of net sales. This figure is representative of many retailing and manufacturing businesses. In our example, net pretax profit after deducting owner salary is $10,000. So we can divide to determine annual net sales:

$$\text{Net sales} = \frac{\$10,000}{5\%} = \frac{\$10,000}{.05} = \$200,000 \text{ per year}$$

The equation for the sales needed each business day to generate our $40,000 income each year is:

$$\text{Needed sales per day} = \frac{\$200,000}{52\text{-week year} \times 6\text{-day week}} = \$640$$

That is, the cash register must ring up $640 each business day of the year, on the average, for the owner to have his or her $30,000 salary and $10,000 return on investment (which, incidentally, will most likely be plowed right back into the business).

Now let's look at the number of customers needed each day to generate a $40,000 income. This, of course, depends to a great extent on the average purchase per customer. In a women's ready-to-wear store this could be $30 or more. In a hardware store, it is probably much lower, let's assume $10. So customers needed per day for these types of retail outlets are:

Woman's apparel: $\dfrac{\$640 \text{ per day}}{\$30 \text{ per customer}} = 21 \text{ customers}$

Hardware store: $\dfrac{\$640 \text{ per day}}{\$10 \text{ per customer}} = 64 \text{ customers}$

These "per day" figures say a lot about what it takes to make a business succeed. An annual sales volume of $200,000 is a small figure in today's world of $1 million-plus celebrity salaries and multibillion-dollar corporations. It's also an abstract figure: $200,000 per year doesn't say much. But $128 profit per day and $640 in sales per day and 20 to 60 customers per day say exactly what is required for sales success.

I strongly recommend that you calculate these figures for your proposed business. They will help you measure your accomplishments as your business progresses.

The Masses Fallacy

Some small business authors make selling sound so easy. Their argument goes like this: There are 220 *million* people in the United States! All it takes to make $100,000 is to sell 100,00 people a product for $3 that has a total out-of-the-door cost to you of $2.

I say, why not make it easy on yourself! To make $100,000 sell the same $2 item to 50,000 people for $4 each! Or go whole hog and sell it to 1,000 people for $100 each. With 220 million people in the United States, it should be easy to sell 1,000. That's only one out of each 220,000 people.

You and I know that this is a pie-in-the-sky approach to selling, because it doesn't address the hard questions. What really is this $2 product, anyway? And why would tens of thousands of people want to shell out $3 for it, anyway?

Don't allow yourself to be caught up in this type of nebulous idea. Taken to it's extreme, it says you can sell your $2 product to one person for $100,000 or to 10 million people for $2.01. But it never specifies the products or the value it delivers to the customer.

SUCCESSFUL SELLING.

Successful selling results from the application of time-tested techniques and methods. Although it is probably true that there is such a being as a born (or natural) salesperson, it is just as true that anyone with the proper attitude and motivation can sell effectively. Let's examine the basics of successful selling.

Knowing Products and Markets

You no doubt already know a great deal about the business environment you are going to enter, either through past experience or through the business analysis you've done to select your specific business opportunity.

This prior knowledge should be used as a base to build upon. One of the most interesting aspects of having a business of your own is the opportunity it affords for continual exposure to new people and new information and new ideas. Knowing your products and market by keeping up on what's going on, makes selling easier.

Join local business organizations such as the chamber of commerce and take an active part in their activities. Local business owners in all lines of business have much in common. Membership will expose you to new opportunities and new approaches that can lead to increased sales.

It's also a good idea to join the trade association that focuses on your particular business type. Trade associations can provide you with product and market information that is not available anywhere else. And membership will put you in direct contact with a group of business owners who share your interests and problems.

Another way to keep up with your business and markets is to read. The *Wall Street Journal* is essential, as a starter. You also should subscribe to some of the major business magazines. I've always found *Forbes* and *Business Week* extremely informative. Finally, subscribe and read (or at least skim) all the trade publications in a particular field. Many are available at no cost.

Some business owners make the mistake of isolating themselves from equipment and merchandise suppliers. Business owners are especially prone to ignore suppliers with whom they have no active dealings. But all suppliers are great sources of information. They know who's buying what, they know about new processes and new merchandise, and they always know a lot about what's going on. Suppliers enjoy discussing their knowledge with customers and potential customers, so have lunch with them once in a while. It may be time well spent.

Above all else, keep up with the needs of your customers, especially if you're serving a commercial market. Try to know your customers' business as well as they do. It's important to convey a genuine concern about your customers' problems. They should feel that they can confide in you. It could well be that a customer's problem will become an attractive new product or service opportunity for you.

Try to remember to keep your information-seeking horizons broad. Selling success encompasses attention to all marketing and sales activities, including marketing research and marketing planning. In retailing, it means attention to advertising, promotion, store design and layout, store appearance, displays, in-store promotions, and all aspects of customer contact. In industrial selling or wholeselling, it means getting the most out of calls on engineers, purchasing agents, and buyers.

Adjusting to the Situation

What would you do in this situation? Say you've been out of work. You're in debt. The only job you've been offered is as a new car salesman. The pay is straight commission, and you get fired if you don't outperform the dealership's top salesperson within 60 days. And the dealer says, "And you get no floor time." This means that you'll get no walk-in business. You'll have to hustle it up somewhere else.

This is the situation that confronted Joe Giradi, and from this situation he went on to become the best car salesman of all times. His earnings reached $150,000 to $200,000 per year. He sells over 100 cars a month—more than a lot of dealerships. How did he do it? Partly on drive and perseverance, partly by adapting to the situation. He offered his customers the best deal in town by cutting his commission to the bone. Then he let it be known that he would pay anybody $25 if they sent a customer his way. He has happily paid out as much as $14,000 in 1 year to his "bird dogs."

In the first several months Joe went out and made his pitch to everyone he knew. Some bought. Others bird-dogged. All were happy. Joe's car sales volume quickly satisfied his dealer's prior conditions, and in no time he was making thousands of dollars a month on sheer volume. As the word spread, customers were coming to him from hundreds of miles away.

Joe's experience is a beautiful example of what I mean by adjusting to the situation. Selling requires flexibility and creative thinking to match your products or services to customers' wants and needs.

Self-confidence and Enthusiasm

New insurance salespersons are told to expect to fail 9 out of 10 times. They are also taught not to be disheartened by 20 or even 30 failures in a row, because *on the average* they can expect to sell 1 out of 10. After coming up dry 30 times, they may hit 4 out of the next 10.

All this statistical information is aimed at helping insurance salesmen maintain self-confidence when confronted with one failure after another. This is critical, because a person who feels that he or she is going to succeed is more likely to succeed. And a person with self-doubts brings those feelings to the selling interface where they often prove to be a seller's downfall.

Enthusiasm shows. And it helps sell products and services. Of course, the best enthusiasm is genuine enthusiasm. And this comes from being in a business that one enjoys, and from knowing the benefits and advantages of the product or service being offered.

Nothing is worse than trying to sell a product or service that you don't believe in. I've been in that situation in industry. I didn't enjoy it, and my lack of enthusiasm for the products showed in my sales results. Remember this when you choose a business and when you have a chance to diversify or take on a new product line. If you don't believe in what you're doing, why should customers believe in you?

Preparation

Abraham Lincoln once said, "When I'm getting ready to reason with a man, I spend one-third of my time thinking about myself and what I'm going to say—and two-thirds thinking about him and what he is going to say." This approach is directly applicable to the selling situation. In fact, effective selling has quite a lot in common with reasoning.

The emphasis on preparation is also apparent in the quote from Lincoln. A logical corollary to it (for a selling situation) might be a statement like this: The time spent preparing for selling contributes more to closing a sale than the time spent with the customer. The truth in this statement is apparent when you consider all the effort that should go into preparation for selling. Here are some major considerations:

For retail selling	For industrial or wholesale selling
• Advertising	• Specifications
• Signs and banners	• Price lists
• Point-of-sale markers	• Catalogs
• Promotions	• Brochures
• Mailings	• Samples
• Salesperson training	• Presentations
• Recording the sale	

Preparation also contributes to self-confidence and enthusiasm.

Specific Selling Techniques

A number of selling techniques can be very useful in improving sales effectiveness. These include:

- Prospecting techniques
- Methods of approach
- Presentation skills (e.g., eye contact)
- Ways of overcoming objections
- Closing techniques

There are tons of information available on these techniques—cassette training courses, seminars, and books. Some of this stuff is good, even invaluable, but the rest is a rip-off. Be selective in what you buy, but do make a commitment to improve your selling techniques and skills.

A good place to start is the books on salesmanship in your local library. Most of these are written by veterans of the selling trade. When reading them begins to get repetitious, you'll know that you've read enough. Then it's time to put into practice the techniques that will help you to be a selling success.

Viewing one's business from the perspective of customers and potential customers is another powerful selling tool. It's unfortunate that more small business owners don't utilize it to its fullest advantage.

Customers and potential customers communicate with business owners through their actions or inactions as well as with words. Usually what they do or don't do means more than what they say.

A FINAL WORD.

This is the end of *Straight Talk.* I've discussed candidly the risks and pitfalls as well as the profits and rewards of owning and managing a small business. Now you should be able to make an enlightened decision concerning your future. And if you do decide to join the ranks of the self-employed, I hope that the information and insights I have offered in this book will be truly helpful. Thanks for reading it.

APPENDIX

New product analysis and testing.

The following material is taken from *The Handbook of Business Problem Solving*. It demonstrates the cautious (yet not always successful) approach that large corporations use to develop new products.[1] This chapter is intended to provide an overview of the entire new product developmental process, from the inception of an idea to the national launching of a totally new product.

In general, the marketing of new products can be described as a four-phase process:

- Concept development and testing
- Prototype and "protocept" development and testing
- Market planning and testing
- Broadscale expansion and monitoring

Not all new products will follow each phase with equal intensity or sophistication. The relative weights given to factors such as competitive and financial risk will often determine the emphasis upon each phase of a project.

[1] Chapter 4-2, by Lynn X. Y. Lin, Ph.D., William J. McKenna, Reg Rhodes, and Steve Wilson (vice-presidents of Booz, Allen & Hamilton, Inc.), in *The Handbook of Business Problem Solving*, Kenneth J. Albert (Ed.-in-chief), McGraw-Hill, 1980.

However, experience would clearly indicate that each phase should be addressed during decision making, even if the entire process is being balanced against informal judgment or entrepreneurial "gut feel." As an assist in utilizing the four-phase new product planning process, each phase had been expanded into the decision-making system flowchart in Figure 1.

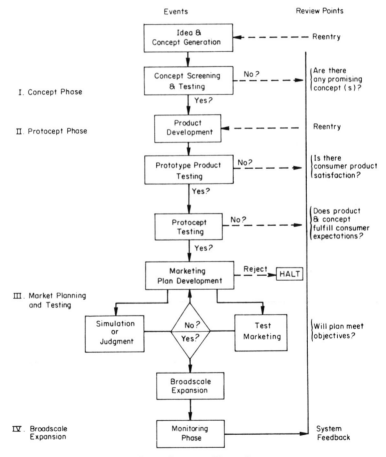

Figure 1   Decision-making System Flowchart

IDEA AND CONCEPT GENERATION.

New product ideas or concepts are secured from a wide variety of sources. The principal sources for consumer package goods are as follows:

- R&D laboratories
- Consumers
- Analysis of historical data
- Outside consultants

Each of these sources has consistently produced ideas that have resulted in successful new products. How well competing firms manage their sources of new product ideas will often determine future market leadership.

R&D Laboratories

R&D is critically important to new products since it must ultimately execute the firm's new product ideas, whether generated internally or provided from other sources. R&D is expected to be aware of the latest technology on formulation, packaging, and manufacturing. When confronted with emerging technology, R&D may expand its ranks with additional staff or secure specialized outside consulting assistance.

As an example, in the health and beauty aids field the R&D department is most often the source of new concepts or ideas. The capabilities of modern chemistry are mostly unknown to consumers, and so the lab must continually work to improve the performance of existing products. The "wet look" in lipstick was not a need verbalized by consumers, but rather a technology-based product difference that made many women "feel prettier" and thus started a fashion trend. The shampoo and hair conditioner markets have evolved in much the same way, with lab-generated concepts such as proper pH level and protein content.

Consumers

The consumer can provide new product ideas in many ways, including the following:

- Voluntary suggestion letters
- Consumer contests
- Consumer research studies

A great number of recipes and actual product-usage information voluntarily provided to manufacturers by consumers serve as the basis for new products. This is particularly true of prepared food items and mixes. Often the manufacturer aggressively pursues ideas through baking and recipe contests.

The multimillion-dollar marketing research industry experiences a considerable amount of client activity that centers on talking to individual or small groups of consumers about their experiences in designated product-usage areas. These interviews, called "depth interviews" on an individual basis and "focus groups" when they involve approximately seven to ten consumers in a single session, attempt to probe consumer attitudes in specific areas of behavior. These attitudes include general likes and dislikes about available products and brands. Highly skilled interviewers attempt to probe deeply into these attitudes to find voids or gaps in the fulfillment of consumer needs that might be satisfied by introducing a new product.

New product marketing personnel participate in these interviews by viewing the interview live from a remote location or, if unable to do this, listening to audio tapes of the interviews. In this manner, they use the consumer interview as a stimulant in forming hypotheses that might soon spawn one or more new product ideas.

Some firms conduct statistically projectable studies among large samples of the consumer population in order to add objectivity and significance to the new product ideation process. Techniques such as multivariate, product gap, and tradeoff analysis have proved useful in quantifying consumers' needs for product characteristics that are yet unfulfilled by available products.

Analysis of Historical Data

An in-depth inspection of historical demographic and social (lifestyle) trends would explain many of the current sales trends in our consumer product markets. For example, rapidly increasing numbers of working women and smaller families with multiple wage earners might indicate that the consumer will be more receptive to a new adult-oriented convenience food. This same trend might tell a household-products manufacturer that a new furniture polish or window cleaning fluid might be targeted toward an increasingly uninterested consumer.

Source documents for these analyses are often found in the public sector since they are often sponsored by the government. Census reports and studies conducted by various other federal agencies, such as the Food and Drug Administration (FDA), the U.S. Department of Agriculture (USDA), and the Department of Health, Education and Welfare (HEW), contain extensive information on social trends and changes in consumer attitudes over time.

In some instances, analyzing behavioral data from other technologically advanced societies will provide the basic idea for a new United States product. For example, Clairol's Herbal Essence Shampoo was reportedly derived from interviews with American women who had been living in Europe and were preparing to return to the United States. Respondents were asked about items they would miss because they were not available in the United States. A herbal shampoo that was popular in Europe was frequently associated with a strong sense of loss.

CONCEPT SCREENING AND TESTING.

After new product concepts have been generated, the next step is to evaluate them, both internally and externally. The internal evaluation generally precedes external evaluation by consumers, and focuses on the following issues:

- Available technology
- Potential business size

- Production capacity
- Capital investment and asset utilization
- Marketplace factors (channel access, likely competition, uniqueness)

Concepts that survive this stage will be released for external screening by consumers.

The external evaluation attempts to reduce the number of alternative product concepts on the basis of consumer interest. At this point in the developmental process spending is a small percentage (less than 5 percent) of total expenditures needed to achieve broad-scale expansion. Thus, it is critically important to perform concept tests among target groups of consumers before proceeding into heavy R&D and market research expenditures.

The concept test will generally utilize consumer "like/dislike" and "intent-to-buy" scores to screen out low-interest concepts. Concepts can either be alternative positionings within a single new product area or a mixture of concepts from several new product areas. In the latter type of test, one must be mindful of committing a "type II error," i.e., rejecting a powerful concept in a medium-size product category simply because competing concepts were from larger categories.

Concept tests are generally performed in one of two ways: by mail or through personal interviews. To conduct a test by mail, one would mail to randomly chosen consumers (approximately 500) anywhere from one to six concept cards (including the test concept) and a questionnaire with some incentive for returning it completed. Personal interviews can be conducted either by applying the identical procedure to a central location (e.g., shopping mall intercept) or in the consumers' homes.

Personal interviews in a central location are used most often due to convenience, accuracy, and cost savings. Standard test sample sizes range from 100 to 1000 per concept, averaging approximately 300 per concept. It is important to note here that more than one concept (e.g., two different positionings or unit prices) for the same product should not be viewed by the same respondent. The concept statement card used for this test is generally in a very crude, raw form with no brand name or fancy package included.

Key measurements in this concept test, in addition to some necessary demographic and general-usage information, are purchase intent, frequency of use, and competitive information. Questions concerning the competitive environment may cover the replacement of currently used products and brands by the new product, and how the product's future use pattern is perceived, i.e., exclusively or interchangeably with other brands. The purchase intent question should be asked prior to eliciting any usage and product attribute responses in order to avoid excessive exaggeration by consumers.

Analysis of the concept-screening data will generally focus on an evaluation of purchase intent scores. The commonly used purchase intent measure is a five-point scale (definitely would, probably would, may or may not, probably would not, and definitely would not buy).

There are as many ways to evaluate the meaning of the purchase intent response as there are market researchers and product categories. However, marketers most often will use past experience in tracking consumer response from the concept stage through actual purchase behavior in order to develop their own weighing scheme for purchase intent responses to use in estimating first-year trial rates. Surprisingly, this estimation made from consumer response (future purchase intent) has proved, in the experience of both the author and several others, to be fairly accurate in predicting future purchase behavior. The following table illustrates four weighing schemes commonly used by market research professionals:

Purchase intent	1	2	3	4
Defintely would buy	100%	52%	100%	90%
Probably would buy	0	17	40	30
May or may not buy	0	8	0	5
Probably would not buy	0	2	0	2.5
Definitely would not buy	0	1	0	2

Which weighing scheme to use depends on the product category. Past experience also indicates that a product's potential purchase cycle should influence the weights. In general, the shorter the purchase cycle the closer consumer response is to actual behavior, thus shifting the weight upward toward the top box score (definite buy). Later in this chapter, an example will be given that uses weighing scheme 4.

Knowing the appropriate weighing scheme to use on a given project is the most difficult and proprietary part of any firm's concept test analysis. A company with no current entry or behavioral information in a given new product category is sometimes wise to seek assistance from a qualified new product market research firm. It conducts the concept test and, at the same time, provides the first initial trial rate estimate for each product concept. In preparing the first-year trial estimate, one also needs to make adjustments for product all commodity volume (ACV), distribution assumption, awareness levels, and seasonal and regional factors, such as category development index (CDI) or brand development index (BDI).

PRODUCT DEVELOPMENT AND TESTING.

The R&D department will normally be aware of work done during the concept phase. Its involvement during the concept phase is presumed since R&D input on feasibility assessment and planning is essential to a smoothly running new products department. This involvement is usually formalized through committees and regular reporting relationships.

Concepts that survive consumer testing are assigned priorities and scheduled for prototype development. The basis for assigning priorities would include a review of new project requirements and their critical paths, and long-range plans and projects already under development.

Once a new concept product is scheduled for development, continuous management control over the project is provided through project progress and budget performance reports.

The prototype which represents the concept will normally undergo a variety of performance tests before leaving this phase. The initial tests are called product performance tests, and their objective is to determine how well the prototype matches the original concept specifications. Most performance tests are performed on a blind basis, i.e., with packaging but without brand identification or advertising copy, in order to obtain a pure rating on the product. If competitive items are available, then they might also be tested on a blind basis to obtain a comparative measure.

Performance tests would include one or more of the following research design approaches:

- Expert panels
- Central location consumer tests
- Home use tests by consumers

The actual technique utilized in the performance research will vary according to the product category and uniqueness properties of the product being developed. Both comparative and absolute ratings will be obtained during a typical series of performance tests.

Once the product prototype is thought to be completely developed, the concept will be integrated with the prototype to form a "protocept." Concept statements are normally transformed into packaging graphics, brand names, and rough advertising copy statements in preparation for this next stage of protocept development and testing.

PROTOCEPT TESTING.

While our product was being developed by R&D, the brand manager initiated communication research to identify potential selling points for the product and a brand name, if one had not already been selected. Packaging research has also been initiated while R&D was at work. After the brand name, selling points, and package are determined, the R&D prototype is not a protocept that is ready to be tested once again by consumers. The purpose of protocept testing is to estimate both trial and repeat purchase potential of the product.

It is standard procedure for many companies as well as research services to perform protocept tests at a central location similar to the one described for concept tests. Consumers who give purchase intent ratings in the top two boxes are given a prototype product to take home. The reason that only the top two respondent groups are given the product for home use is that these are high-potential triers for the product. To obtain after-use information from them, either a self-administered questionnaire or a telephone callback interview is used. If the telephone callback is used, only a limited number of questions can be effectively asked and some of the rating scales need to be condensed. Self-administered after-use questionnaires are preferred when preparation method or other free response data are desired. Regardless of the data collection technique selected, several key measurements are necessary: purchase intent, future purchase frequency, price value, and like/dislike scores for the new product.

To obtain the potential repeat rate estimate based on the consumer after-use data, some researchers will use a benchmark method while others will use the combined scores of purchase intent, price value, average like/dislike, and other responses. The benchmark method is valuable if the firm has a large in-house data bank with repeat rates and consumer attitude data for similar items.

The combined attitudinal response method involves modeling new product attitudinal and actual diary repeat data through multiple regression analysis to estimate average repeat potential. The estimation of repeat rate utilizing this method has provided a high degree of accuracy for many consumer packaged goods products.[2]

SIMULATED TEST MARKET OR LABORATORY TEST MARKET.

Once our new product is available for retail sales testing, many large companies will perform a final screening test of the product's vitality

[2] For example, Booz, Allen & Hamilton's BASES model validation has shown some very convincing results.

before test-marketing. These firms, as well as several market research firms, have developed test market laboratory techniques. The lab may utilize either an actual or a simulated store environment. The lab method will utilize a computerized sales volume forecasting model that converts the laboratory behavior of consumers to estimates of first-year sales volume. The current trend is toward increased use of computerized model estimates for final testing before large-scale test-marketing. In general, validation of new product plans through models has proved to be valuable in reducing risk and improving accuracy.[3]

Several research suppliers provide the laboratory type of store-testing facility, such as Yankelovich Laboratory Test Market (LTM) and Management Decision Systems (MDS). The research companies that conduct actual in-store testing include Booz, Allen (Marketing Services group) and National Purchase Diary Research Inc. (NPD). Since the Yankelovich, MDS, and NPD services are familiar to many companies, we will describe the well-validated and new Booz, Allen & Hamilton BASES model testing method in more detail.

The BASES model in-store testing method consists of setting up a test facility in actual grocery or drug stores in client-selected markets. A TV or print commercial viewing station is placed at the store entrance. Shoppers are exposed to the commercials and given coupons in order to trace trial purchases. The test product is placed in the store at a prescribed shelf location at the suggested retail price.

The test scheme goes like this. Regular shoppers come into the store and are contacted by one of the test supervisors and asked to participate in the test. If they agree, they view three or four product commercials (including one test product commercial) in a rotating order and are then given booklets of six store coupons (each with 20 percent off the shelf price). Three or four of the coupons are products for which they have just seen commercials. They then do their regular shopping. The numbered coupons are only good for that day and must be returned at the checkout counter whether or not they are

---

[3] See M. J. Naples, "Successful New Products—It's What's Up Front That Counts," presented at Conference Board, Oct. 25, 1977.

redeemed. The test product purchases (or redemptions) are the real trial purchases by the participants and are used as a basis for estimating the trial rate. The adjusting factors obviously will include the coupon value effect, potential distribution build pattern, advertising and promotional programs, and seasonal and regional (CDI or BDI) factors.

The test product purchasers will then be contacted by phone (timing depends on possible usage frequency) and asked about after-use responses which include some key measurements, such as future purchase intent, like/dislike of the product, price value, future purchase frequency, initial purchase units and flavor or size, and other standard questions on product attributes. Based on the telephone callback data, estimated repeat rate, average purchase cycle, and average trial units are obtained. The first-year consumer sales potential is estimated by using the computerized model. It is possible to evaluate marketing alternatives through the simulation of different advertising plans or distribution levels. Sensitivity analysis that provides probability statements or confidence intervals for the sales estimate is the other additional feature of the BASES model.

THE MARKETING PLAN.

After validation of the new product's potential in premarket tests has been completed, it is time to concentrate on the details of marketing the product. The marketing plan is the documentation of all efforts required to market the new product. The marketing plan serves as a key document based on which national introduction and test-marketing activities will be executed. It may be necessary to develop alternative plans if different marketing approaches are contemplated during test-marketing.

A complete marketing plan should include a section outlining the rationale for the new product introduction, financial data (including sales, profit and loss over time), and objectives, strategy, and an execution plan for the following:

- Sell-in, sales promotion, pricing
- Advertising: copy and media
- Consumer promotion

Product Rationale

A rationale statement should be prepared which includes the following.

1. *Review of Product Category and Competition Sales History and Growth Rate*   This should be done for at least the previous five years, for the category in which the new product will compete and for key competitors. Abnormal growth or decline in any of the years should be explained.

Seasonal and regional development should be considered and explained if necessary for both the category and specific brands. Sales should be explained by outlet types (food stores, drug stores, mass merchandiser, or other type). Outlet importance may vary dramatically by brand or manufacturer.

Category consumers should be described by sex, age, and any other relevant demographic criteria. If possible, some attention should be given to the dependence on heavy, medium, and light users of the category. The product category should also be described in terms of brand positioning or segments. For example, the dentifrice category could be divided into therapeutic and cosmetic segments with each brand establishing some relatively unique position or image within each segment.

2. *Rationale and Position of New Product.*   The rationale for introducing the new product should be clearly explained, as should how the new product will be positioned and how it will fit into the existing category. Points of uniqueness and other competitive strengths should be highlighted.

3. *Test Experience.*   Available test results should be outlined. Concept tests, product use tests, new product simulation model results or previous test-market data should be capsulized. Both positive and negative results should be included.

It may be necessary to employ a large number of exhibits for the purposes of brevity in this section of the plan.

Sales and Profit and Loss Over Time

To most readers of a new product marketing plan, the financial data of sales profit and loss (P&L) offer a good overview of key elements surrounding the new product introduction. Reviewing financial data allows the reader to determine the market size of the product discussed, the level of risk involved with the introduction, the level of consumer marketing support required to compete in the category, and the long-range contribution the product may make toward company profits.

Elements necessarily detailed in a marketing plan P&L are:

- Factory sales
- Cost of goods
- Other fixed expenses
- Gross profit
- Sales promotion expenditures
- Consumer marketing expenditures
- Advertising
- Consumer promotion
- Other variable expenses
- Profit contribution

The P&L should project performance for at least five years from the time of introduction.

It will probably also be necessary to elaborate on the factory sales estimates. The factory sales should be detailed in terms of consumer sales and pipeline sales (sales of product at factory which remain in trade warehouses, not yet sold to consumers). Factory sales of the new product will also need to be detailed by size, type, flavor, etc.

Two critical points on a five-year new product plan are the *payout* and *payback* points. A brand is at a payout point when it begins to return a profit and is at a payback point when introductory losses have been fully recovered. Most manufacturers have new product charters which stipulate limits of payout and payback which are acceptable for new product investment. Also, criteria are generally established for profitability once a payout position is reached.

Alternative plans, taking variations in spending levels into account, should be considered. If alternative plans are to be tested, rationale and details for all plans should be set forth in the marketing plans.

Sell-in, Sales Promotion and Pricing

Objectives should be established with regard to distribution (timing and penetration, retail merchandising, and pricing. Objectives should be specific enough to be able to compare against measured performance levels. A simplified example is outlined below.

Sales Objectives

1. The brand will achieve the following levels of distribution:

Month	Food, %	Drug, %	MM, %
3	60	40	30
6	75	60	40
9	85	70	50
12	95	80	60

2. The introductory trial size display unit will be placed in 30 percent of food stores, 25 percent of drug stores, and 20 percent of mass merchandisers.

3. Average retail prices will be as follows:

Size	Introduction (3 mo)			Every day		
	Food	Drug	MM	Food	Drug	MM
1	$ .80	$ .85	$ .80	$1.00	$1.10	$1.00
2	1.50	1.65	1.50	1.70	1.85	1.70

A strategy statement, a simplified example of which follows, should be prepared to accomplish the objectives.

Sales Strategy

1.   A combination of direct sales personnel and food brokers will be used during the introduction (year 1). Direct personnel will concentrate on major accounts; brokers will concentrate on small- to medium-sized accounts.

2.   Trial size displays will be sold to the trade, offering 80 percent profit, to solicit immediate purchase and distribution. Supplementary retail personnel will be used to assure retail setup of display units.

3.   Heavy off-invoice promotion will be offered during the introduction to achieve initial low prices. Return to standard margins will lead to anticipated regular prices.

Finally, a detailed plan is needed to specify critical details of:

1.   Sales force composition

2.   Product introduction to sales force (introductory meetings)

3.   Timing to sell-in

4.   Introductory deal specifications

5.   Year 1 trade deal structure and schedule

6.   Pricing including wholesaler prices

Further, a year 1 sales promotion budget should be set forth. Costs of dealing, sales meetings, selling materials, special packs, etc., should all be included.

Advertising

Advertising can be separated into two distinct segments: copy and media.

Copy   In any copy development plan, it is important for the client (manufacturer) to prepare clear objectives for the advertising agency. The objectives should be derived from sound research that the client has conducted.

The agency, in conjunction with the client, should establish a copy of strategy to which subsequent copy will be written and will conform.

Usually, advertising copy should be decided upon before a marketing plan is written and should be available for inclusion.

All three of the above—copy objectives, copy strategy, and copy for all media (print, radio, TV, other)—should be in the marketing plan. Inclusion of details regarding subsequent copy development plans is optional.

Media   Media plans are prepared similarly to copy, although agency involvement is generally much greater at the beginning. Objectives and strategy should be outlined in the marketing plan, followed by a detailed summary of expenditures by media type (TV, radio, print, etc.) and specifics within type (dayparts, magazine versus newspaper, network versus spot, etc.) Further, expenditures should be outlined by quarter and, if possible, by mouth.

The plan should identify the media target and provide measures of impact against the target and population in general. Reach, frequency, impressions, and GRP's should be discussed.

It is also helpful to provide competitive media programs and advertising/sales ratios for the category and competition to allow readers a perspective on the media plan.

Consumer Promotion

Objectives and strategy should again be specified. Plan elements should be described in detail and may include any or a combination of the following types of support:

1. Couponing
2. Sampling or trial size
3. Demonstrations
4. Cash refunds
5. Premium offers
6. Sweepstakes, contests, etc.

Parameters should be placed on cost and penetration levels of each program. Usually, any significant consumer promotion will be the subject of a detailed document, separate from the marketing plan, which may be appended for elaboration.

The work and thought of many people go into the preparing of a marketing plan. An individual cannot simply sit down and write one. Product cost estimates must be obtained from manufacturing departments. Sales force support and counsel are needed to formulate a sell-in and trade promotion plan. Copy is usually a long laborious process from creation through many levels of legal and management clearance. Media plans require significant attention from agency media departments. The marketing plan basically collects and documents the finished products from all these processes and, one hopes, coordinates the individual elements into a unified support program for a new product introduction.

Once the marketing plan is prepared, if the product is to be test-marketed, the plan must be accurately translated into the test area. Translation of a national plan to a test situation is difficult and requires experience. Straight-line translation is seldom the rule; experience will, however, suggest rules of thumb for most elments included in a plan.

TEST-MARKETING.

The new product marketing process has now reached the stage where introduction to the marketplace with full marketing support is all that remains. The scope of an introduction at this stage is usually limited to small geographic areas labeled test markets. The purpose of test-marketing includes the following:

- *Minimize the Risk* of financial loss and loss of image with customers resulting from a new product failure.
- *Optimize the Sales* potential for the new product by testing alternative plans, i.e., shifting spending levels and priorities within the marketing mix.

The value of test-marketing is clearly evidenced by the number of successful new consumer products whose marketing plans for national introduction changed substantially following test-marketing.

Firms who do not test-market their new products are often concerned about the loss of competitive edge that could result from testing in an environment where competing firms will monitor your new brand's progress. If the new product formulation and packaging are easily duplicated, then perhaps a competitor, sensing success, can and will steal the initiative by introducing a similar product nationally while the innovator's brand is still in test-marketing. Many health and beauty aids (HBA) new product introductions were never test-marketed as a result of this concern.

However, for most firms, the minimization of financial risk takes precedence over fear of competitive preemption, and test-marketing is a necessary step. "Minimarketing," which is described later in the chapter, offers several advantages to the marketer who want to test-market but needs quick answers and maximum security.

A "conventional" test market usually consists of two or three sales districts covering anywhere from 2 to 6 percent of the United States population. Sales force sell-in to the retail trade replicates in almost all respects the brands national marketing plan. The test-market selection process usually involves screening against one or more of the following criteria:

- Demographics/projectable consumer environment
- Sales force capability/trade factors
- Brand and category development for competing brands
- Media coverage and spill-out considerations
- Cost of media, research, and promotion

Test-market sales measurement usually spans from six months to one or more years and involves utilization of the following research sales data collection techniques.

- Store audits
- Warehouse withdrawals
- Consumer diary panels
- Factory shipments
- Telephone interviews

Sales projections can and are routinely made from each of the aforementioned sources. However, in the package goods field, *consumer diary panels* are recognized as preeminent in their ability to accurately predict future sales of a new product. The reason for this acclaim lies in the nature of a package good, that is, its dependence upon *repeat purchasing* by triers to achieve stable or increasing long-term sales. As discussed earlier in concept and protocept testing, the repeat-purchase factor is the most critical in determining long-term viability. Diary panels, where groups of consumers maintain continuous records of purchasing, represent the needed data base of triers and their post-trial purchases (repeats).

There are several sales projection models using trial and repeat-purchase data. Most of these models succeed in providing improved forecasts of long-term new product sales volume and share. The Booz, Allen & Hamilton model mentioned previously offers a dynamic simulation capability in addition to basic sales tracking and projection. Brand managers can vary the level and timing of applications for each marketing variable and provide updated forecasts when marketing plan changes are made.

For the marketer who is concerned about the high cost and lack of secrecy in conventional test markets, minimarkets, as small controlled test markets are called, offer an alternative with many advantages and only a few limitations.

Minimarketing was pioneered in the late 1960s by three research firms: Market Audits (Booz, Allen & Hamilton), Burgoynne, and Market Facts. Since then, several other firms, such as A. C. Nielsen and AdTel (Booz, Allen & Hamilton), have successfully entered the field.

The main distinguishing features of minimarkets are as follows:

- Controlled store placements
- Research firm acts as manufacturer's sales force, thereby eliminating burden on established brand sales force.
- Research firm agreements with retailer will ensure replication of marketing plan during the test.

- Small and well-isolated market
- Minimal spill-in and spill-out of media and promotion
- Low competitive visibility, making it difficult for competitors to measure
- Lower cost
- Ability to test alternative marketing plans
- Advertising (copy, spending level, scheduling)
- Promotion (coupon, sample)
- Pricing and shelf placement

Major test-marketing research firms have established their own list of minimarkets and can offer testing services in many markets on an exclusive basis.

In minimarkets, the research firm controlling distribution for the test brand can test alternative retail promotions and measure their effect through matched store audit panels. For example, in a thirty-store minimarket test, one might reduce the shelf price and place displays in ten stores, reduce the price only in another ten stores, and do nothing in the ten-store balance or control group. The audit firm will collect sales data for the test brand and competing brands to determine the promotion's effect.

The use of sales projection models with minimarket, diary panel, and store audit data as inputs represents the most accurate and efficient way to test new package goods. Through their use, the new product knowledge gap between large and small firms has narrowed and the overall success rate of new products has increased.

MONITORING EXPANSION MARKETS.

Considering the magnitude of the investment and the risks involved in a major new product launch, it is surprising how frequently the fundamentals of monitoring expansion markets are forgotten or simply overlooked. It would seem as though some marketing and research managers look upon test-market experience as totally predictive and ignore certain obvious facts.

- Controlling product quality on limited runs necessary to support test markets frequently becomes a more difficult task on the larger runs necessary to support large-scale roll-outs. Frequently several plants are involved, substantially increasing the odds that quality and uniformity problems could occur.
- Sales force performance in test markets—subjected to continuous scrutiny from headquarters—can be significantly different from the performance one would reasonably expect during a large-scale roll-out.
- Awareness build—Even if the copy and media delivery are expected to be exactly the same—can also vary from test market to expansion market. For example, if the distribution build pattern changes or the quality or timing of trade merchandising support changes, significant awareness levels are likely to change as well.
- Major elements of the marketing plan are frequently changed once expansion has taken place. This raises the obvious question of what sales effects result from the summation of these changes.

The experience of a major household-products manufacturer illustrates how difficult potential quality control problems can be to anticipate and the value of checking product quality after distribution into expansion markets. In this case, a powdered household product was thoroughly test-marketed on the West Coast. The test-market research cost about $250,000 and included store audits, diary panel data to measure trial and repeat levels, and several waves of central location telephone interviews, which were used to track advertising awareness levels and other diagnostics. Additional qualitative information was obtained from focused group interviews among triers, rejectors, and nontriers. It is doubtful many roll-out decisions have been supported with a greater wealth of positive test-market information. However, as it sometimes the case, the expansion into the Southeastern United States did not include a thorough monitoring plan.

Four months into the expansion, the test-brand share was 25 percent under the comparable test-market share. Recognizing a serious problem, the company made a major effort to identify its source. The test market was initially suspected of being atypical, because in the expansion markets distribution levels were high, out-of-stock conditions were not excessive, and there was an absence of unusually strong competitive activity.

A quality-control check was finally implemented; the test product was picked up from a random sample of store shelves in the expansion markets. It was immediately noticed that the powdered cleaner was lumping and did not pour easily from the container—a problem that was eventually related to high humidity. The problem had not surfaced in the West Coast test market because relative humidity there is significantly lower throughout the year than in the Southeast. Unfortunately, this product-quality problem was not identified until five months after opening expansion markets. A simple formula change did not begin to appear on store shelves for two additional months. This situation is not unique. In many instances the cause of under- or overperformance by brands during expansion might be due to variables not related to the product, such as distribution, competition reaction, and general economic trends. Expansion monitoring of key phases of the test-brand marketing plan is essential regardless of test-market experience.

The monitoring system need not be extravagant or necessarily duplicate the apparatus and expense of the test-market plan. It might consist only of purchasing regional samples of national research services to track sales, distribution, and awareness build. Random samples of retail merchandise would routinely be sent to R&D for performance and quality tests. Sales managers would monitor account authorizations and estimate distribution levels and timing. Awareness build would be tracked through telephone interviews to ensure that trial potential is equal to plan. These data would be used as updated inputs to a sales projection model in order to refine and revise test-market forecasts. In this environment, the brand manager would have full control over the marketing plan.

Index.

DATE			
DEC 1 '82			
JUN 1 '83			
FEB 15 '90			
NOV 21 '94			
DEC 06 '94			
DEC 7 '95			
AUG 12 '96			
MAR 0 9 1998			